Ethical Resources
for Political and Economic Decision

Books by HARVEY SEIFERT
Published by THE WESTMINSTER PRESS

Ethical Resources for Political and Economic Decision
Power Where the Action Is
Conquest by Suffering: The Process and Prospects
of Nonviolent Resistance

In Collaboration with Howard J. Clinebell, Jr.
Personal Growth and Social Change: A Guide
for Ministers and Laymen as Change Agents

Ethical Resources
for
Political and Economic Decision

by HARVEY SEIFERT

THE WESTMINSTER PRESS

Philadelphia

Scripture quotations from the Revised Standard Version of
the Bible are copyright, 1946 and 1952, by the Division of
Christian Education of the National Council of Churches,
and are used by permission.

PUBLISHED BY THE WESTMINSTER PRESS®
PHILADELPHIA, PENNSYLVANIA

PRINTED IN THE UNITED STATES OF AMERICA

Library of Congress Cataloging in Publication Data

Seifert, Harvey.
  Ethical resources for political and economic decision.

  Includes bibliographical references.
  1. United States—Economic policy—1971– 2. United States—
Politics and government—1969– 3. Social ethics. I. Title.
HC106.6.S4   301.5'1   72–1409
ISBN 0–664–20948–3

CONTENTS

PREFACE

WORLD PEACE, race prejudice, and environmental pollution are concerns involving moral and ethical issues that recently have received a great deal of attention. Yet no one of these can be solved without basic economic changes, supported by appropriate political arrangements. The complexity of these politico-economic issues demands particular clarity in analysis, yet they are persistently clouded by controversy. We need to take a hard look at the economic and political alternatives open to the American people and to find some ethical guidelines for national decision.

In this book I have tried to cover the central issues before us, including possibilities and weaknesses of our present structures, radical options reflected in modern extremisms, important programs for improvement, and implications for conflicting life-styles. I have tried to keep the treatment serious enough to speak to specialized students in both ethics and the relevant social sciences. Unless these two interests are related on the level of public policy, we can only choose between the twin tragedies of programs without evaluated goals or sublime purposes without realistic support.

At the same time I have tried to speak understandably to thoughtful citizens, who must make the decisions, whether they be interested in humanistic ethics, or in religion, or simply in survival. New ideas need not only be produced but also popularized. By unfamiliar words and involved sentences, scholars may maintain an aristocracy in which they talk only to each other. I have made the effort, however ungracefully, to keep one foot in the library and the other on the street. I have studied at the London School of Economics, taught undergraduate courses in economics and sociology, and spent a lifetime specializing in social ethics; but at the same time I have been active as a citizen and a churchman.

On economic and political matters we stand in the last stages of a major transition that could lead either to tragedy or to a richer life for all. This book is therefore something of a tract as well as mostly a text. I have added feeling to facts, not to distort the rational observation of data and analysis of issues, but to reinforce the need for study and decision.

I now also acknowledge part of my own social dependence and ethical obligation. Brevity (for the sake of the reader) must not obscure the depth of my gratitude (for the sake of those mentioned), particularly to Lois, who has brought to our marriage great patience and sympathetic indulgence of my preoccupations, to my students and colleagues at the School of Theology at Claremont and at Claremont Graduate School for repeated alleviation of my ignorance, and to Judy Mangel, Faye Willman, and Barbara Henckel for skillful secretarial attention to the idiosyncrasies of my manuscript.

HARVEY SEIFERT

1
OPTIONS IN FUTURES:
I. A Super-industrial Civilization

ON A VOYAGE TO THE MOON, one can emphasize either the vulnerability of the space capsule or the novelty of view. In describing political and economic possibilities, one can paint either the glowing picture of the utopian oversimplifier or the alarming portrayal provided by the dropout or the doom-sayer. Accuracy requires something of both in a more inclusive composite. While we begin here with the encouraging side of things, in the second chapter, without undue delay, we will introduce some balancing considerations.

SCIENCE AS DREAM

Many now living remember a childhood of kerosene lamps and horse-drawn vehicles on muddy roads. In a single generation we have moved to supersonic planes, computers, and television transmission from outer space. Realistic science projects fantastic dreams for the future. By stimulating the brain electronically or chemically we can already modify behavior. By "genetic surgery" we may soon produce the kind of human beings we want, populating the earth with either Napoleons or St. Francises. Within the next century we are likely to move into the sea and the sky, making both part of our native habitat. The tremendous acceleration in invention leads one economist to suggest that "as far as many statistical series related to activities of mankind are concerned, the date that divides human history into two equal parts is well within living memory." [1] In these respects roughly as much has happened since we were born as had happened before. Of all the scientists who ever lived, at least half are alive today. In some fields the sum total of human knowledge is doubling every five or six years. Irving Kaplan, a psychologist much concerned about the impact of computers, projects the possibility of more technological progress in the next twenty years than in the previous two million.[2] Alvin Toffler speaks of "future shock," an intense disorientation due to great rapidity of change. This is the kind of culture shock travelers have felt as they dropped into a completely different society—except that now all of us experience such shock by simply staying home and living a year longer.[3]

Technological progress has been associated with important nonmaterial gains. The total economic product has included an increasing proportion of services. Not only are essentials of food, clothing, and shelter more available, but also the help of physicians, priests, and professional leaders for rocket societies and Campfire Girls, or national park rangers and travel agents, or business consultants and adult education teachers. In advanced industrial nations the modern workingman lives on a higher level than did medieval kings. If anyone doubts this, he ought to try living in an unmodernized castle without medical specialists! Economic productivity plus democratic political aspirations have provided more for all classes in our own country and promise more for men everywhere. Arnold Toynbee has suggested that ours may be the first generation in history to take seriously the possibility of the good life for every man on earth. In a significant expansion of the borders of human community, we now have the technological basis for the birthday of the world.

Many of these benefits are being made available with less labor. Machines have made possible astonishing increases in productivity per man-hour. Automation may go a long way toward freeing mankind from drudgery as well as want. Four-day workweeks and longer annual vacations are increasingly available. New ways of retarding the aging process, as well as increased leisure, may allow more people to have a double vocation. In addition to their first career they may have time for another occupation that they have always wanted to pursue. What are the possibilities here for greatly increasing the number of paramedical assistants, church workers, or social service trainees?

Another trend that may be extended into the future is increased freedom from autocratic controls. In spite of glaring exceptions, democratic societies provide greater political freedom than was ever enjoyed by ancient slaves or medieval serfs. The common man has wider access to the decision-making process. The extension of the vote to younger adults is a recent step comparable to the vote won earlier for women. In comparison with the past, labor unions have a great deal to say about conditions of work. New meanings may still be given to participatory democracy and anticipatory democracy. The first of these would share more power with the powerless. The second would introduce new ranges of public decision by planning goals for more distant futures. With all of its limitations, our society, in comparison with more totalitarian systems, has been moving toward the promise of such freedoms. Those who describe the United States as a repressive dictatorship have never lived under a Hitler or a Stalin!

The accomplishments of the past allow a new concentration on the higher potentialities of human life. We are now approaching the end of the major preoccupation of humanity during all its previous existence—the preoccupation with material needs. It was to the production and distribution of material goods that men during past centuries gave most of their waking hours and the bulk of their creative energy. In industrially developed regions we have now moved into a comparative age of affluence from the times of scarcity that had existed from the dawn of human history. In geographic areas less well developed, we now know how adequacy, at least, can be achieved.

An era of such comparative realization of the top human priorities is a threatening as well as a promising time for many people. From his monumental studies Arnold Toynbee concluded that civilizations remain viable only so long as they are creatively responding to a challenge.[4] When the accepted challenge disappears, civilizations collapse. Now that the central challenge of material necessity no longer has the same force, if we simply devote ourselves to enjoying the achievements of our forefathers, we can expect only the disintegration of our culture. For both individuals and societies, health requires growth. Strength and competence come only through meeting difficulties. Contentment born of affluence tends to stifle creativity. A passively prosperous population promotes the collapse of civilization, because it will not deal with the strains and contradictions that continue to exist on a nonmaterial level.

We now need a new preoccupation to propel us into the future and to do for us what economic scarcity did in the preceding history of mankind. To understand what this preoccupation might be, consider the classification of values often proposed by the philosophical ethicist. This places physical and material values at the bottom of the scale, social values in intermediate position, and spiritual (i.e., intellectual, aesthetic, moral, and religious) values at the top. It becomes the privilege of the present generation in its major priorities to move from traditional emphases on lower values to a greater preoccupation with social and spiritual values. Ours can now become more humanistic and democratic goals. The great concerns enlisting our best energies would then include improvement in social relationships to uncover the power in intimacy in mass society, or to find solutions to persisting problems like racism, war, conflict between the generations, crime, pollution, or economic injustice. We might also make unprecedented discoveries by focusing more largely on moral, aesthetic, and religious realms. What might we learn, for example, about the meaning of love, the power of beauty, the possibilities in extrasensory perception, the relationship of religion to health, or the meaning of life? In the past few decades there has already been an astonishing increase in the number of symphony orchestras and local theater groups in the United States. A single performance of *Hamlet* on a national network now reaches more people than all the previous presentations of the play from Shakespeare's day to our own. Can we look forward to folk-art galleries in every neighborhood and amateur musical groups scattered through every town? May persons turn to ethical advisers even as they now go to doctors? Will psychological growth groups and prayer retreats become as popular as Disneyland and ski resorts?

Civilization does not continue indefinitely to become better because its physical products are bigger, newer, or richer. Progress must now come to be defined in terms of full human actualization. Each human being now uses only a tiny fraction of his potentialities. Today's genius may come to be seen as a simpleton as we learn to release long-dormant capabilities of man. Unless we make this transition to a new preoccupation, we are doomed. If we do make this transition, we may reveal a new quality of life. A new human being may emerge, using the best in his tradition in a new historical manifestation. All persons could then have a fresh awakening to values long neglected—the beauty of a rushing stream in the wilderness, poetry and philosophy, music and art, the height of the mountains and the expanse of the ocean, the power that comes from relating life more completely to its ultimate source and destiny in God. (I recognize that the view of the ultimate carried in the concept of God eludes finite comprehension and differs for different people. We may emphasize various aspects of meaning in the concept and yet agree that exploration into the theological dimensions of reality is one of the most exciting prospects before us.) These are future resources that would enrich us beyond any comparison with the existing physical affluence of a modern home or the comforts of a technological society.

Such a shift in our primary attention would result in a new

basis for attributing status and worth. A "leading citizen" in the community would be defined, not as rich or bureaucratically powerful, but as humanly sensitive, socially creative, aesthetically appreciative, and morally and spiritually alert. Similarly, "great powers" among the nations would be designated not because of their military power but because of their ideological and sociological contribution. Presumably this would provide less cause for international conflict. The values over which nations now strive are scarce values; they are diminished when they are divided. When a nation surrenders land or oil rights, it loses them. In contrast, social and spiritual values are abundant values; they are multiplied as they are divided. At the same time that one shares an idea or an appreciation, he can also fully retain it himself. This observation is not to fall into the trap of an untenable utopianism. For a long time to come, nations will still find plenty to fight about, such as the ocean floor, the moon, or economic privilege and political pride. Overpopulation and pollution can prolong or create scarcity in material goods. Yet at some time in the future, if we work our way through these problems and to a greater economic abundance, nations may become comparatively more willing to give the management of oceans and space to the United Nations and to concentrate on higher human potentialities.

In these days when the country is in a depression of the spirit, it is important to remember that this genuine option for the future is tremendously exciting. When it is easy to feel that things are falling apart and that there is nothing to look forward to, we can recall that there are positive trends that are not at all certain but that are possible. They are worth giving life to. We may be on the edge of discoveries regarding social and spiritual realities as amazing as the past advances of physical man. We may move into a super-industrial civilization. Such a civilization would retain the gifts of industrial processes but would no longer be dominated by industrialism. It would relate inventive skills and common purposes to higher values.

The agricultural era stressed human and animal power. The

industrial era added machine power. The super-industrial future may introduce more nonphysical powers of man, related to central, cosmic forces. As the industrial revolution led to the present era, the human revolution may bring us to the next great stage of history. The significance of this may ultimately prove to be so great as to justify comparison not so much with the industrial revolution as with the much earlier beginnings of civilization itself. In the history of man we now stand at the end of the beginning, or as H. G. Wells put it, "the twilight of the dawn." Alvin Toffler summarizes by saying, "A growing body of reputable opinion asserts that the present moment represents nothing less than the second great divide in human history, comparable in magnitude only with that first great break in historic continuity, the shift from barbarism to civilization." [5]

ETHICS AS REALITY

So promising a prospect may be increasingly realized, or it may be completely forfeited. What is likely to make the difference? Scientific discovery and technological development will have an influence, but they will not be primary determinants. They are sources of both promise and peril. They can be used to move us in either direction. Neither will the chief influence be political or economic forms. Both democracy and dictatorship can be used in a reactionary protection of the past and a refusal to face the issues necessary for a viable future. A capitalist society may or may not develop its full capacities for good or evil. A planned economy can be used either for actualizing or desecrating man. The major element in shaping the future is the nature and the degree of commitment to the basic values accepted by a society. The common ethos of a people in the long run modifies its social forms and determines its specific goals. The critical construction of an adequate value system is the contribution of philosophy and religion. Without that contribution it is unlikely that we shall resolve our threatening dilemmas or have any kind of tolerable future. This is one of the inflexible realities of social life.

What Frankl calls a "value vacuum" is especially disastrous for both individuals and society in times of rapid social change involving basic crucial choice. To hold a people together when things are flying apart, to focus energies instead of floundering, we need common reference points, widely shared goals. The shape of things to come is altered by our most compelling aims in the present. What do we want an economic system and related political policies to accomplish? In maximizing the gross national product of goods and services, how do we determine which goods are good and which services actually serve? What are the ends to which they are expected to contribute? In devising a future it makes a great deal of difference whether our actual commitments are to hedonistic escape, or to the comforts of luxury, or to providing opportunity for the poor. We are more likely to move toward a super-industrial civilization if this course of action is supported by the value systems to which we are in actuality connected.

There is considerable divergence in this generation on more specific ethical guidelines that will be considered throughout this book. Yet on general norms or goals that will be elaborated in this chapter, there is widespread theoretical agreement. To be sure, we do not always push beyond vague aspiration to allow these norms to become practically operative as dominant motive. One of our chief assignments will be to make our actual behavior more congruent with our accepted goals. Insofar as we accomplish this, those goals do support the general pattern for a progressive future outlined above. They relate a more liberating and fulfilling future to our most basic convictions about ultimate matters. To a considerable extent these norms were historically stimulated by the Judeo-Christian tradition, which is our national religious heritage. These norms raise warnings about some aspects of our politico-economic life and point new directions for change. They also give to specific measures for social progress the support of our most inclusive conclusions about reality. Making a particular invention or securing a concrete social welfare measure take on new importance when these are related to the total meaning of life, fulfillment for humanity, and the purposes of God.

Whether or not economic activity can be justified at all depends on its contribution to human fulfillment. All political and economic arrangements are to be tested by their effect on persons. They have positive significance only insofar as they contribute to the liberation and nurture of man's highest potentialities. Such a contribution can be made in one of two ways, either through consumption of the products of economic enterprise or through participation in economic production. The first of these incorporates the consumer's interest and the second the worker's interest. The wide sweep of the neglected implications of this common insight suggests a great deal about the direction for economic and political change.

As God's material creation is good, so the products of economic activity can be indispensably important. The counterculture is quite incorrect when it views the Judeo-Christian faith as rejecting the enjoyment of physical reality. The Bible is full of ecstatic delight in the beauty of the world, robust lip-smacking at banquets, and reveling in God's creation. Jesus enjoyed the lilies of the field and the birds in the air and bountiful banquets. This is not a world renouncing religion. Absolute asceticism, in a sense of claiming that material goods must be shunned as evil, is a distortion of the faith. The businessman, therefore, does not need to apologize for dealing with material things. On the contrary, making them available for their purpose is clearly good. All other things being equal, productivity is a value to be prized. It can rescue the starving, liberate the senses, and provide energies for the highest of men's endeavors. A higher standard of living, so long as it does not deprive others, is good.

So long as it provides goods and services necessary for social, intellectual, aesthetic, and spiritual growth, economic activity has religious significance. Managers and engineers cannot claim autonomy or immunity from all moral obligation or ecclesiastical review. Technological decisions cannot escape being ethical decisions. They have to do with the quantity and type of output and with the economy and safety of the process. All of these involve important human values. Brunner pointed out that since all means already incorporate ends, "there are no neutral means; hence there can be no 'purely technical' use of means. . . . It is unpardonably thoughtless to speak of the 'ethical neutrality of technology.' " [6]

Furthermore, a major moral demand is that there should be a realization of higher values. Businessmen, hippies, and all the rest of us mortals need to be repeatedly warned that material goods are not the most important value. If we make them the chief end of life, they become an obstacle to full realization of higher values that are more permanent, more significant, and involve more of potentiality for human growth. It is immoral to make material things ultimate. "A man's life does not consist in the abundance of his possessions." (Luke 12:15.) Jesus warned against laying up treasures on earth at the expense of spiritual fulfillment, observing that "where your treasure is, there will your heart be also" (Matt. 6:19–21). Unless we give social and spiritual values a higher place than material goods, we are placing mammon before God. A mania for things leads to misdirected effort, waste of resources, weakening the ties of community, conflict of all against all for scarce commodities, and obscuring the purpose of life. Plato properly complained about statesmen who "filled the city full of harbors and docks and walls and revenues and such trifles to the exclusion of temperance and righteousness." "Fool" is the Scriptural designation for one who destroys personhood to preserve possessions (Luke 12:20).

Some material goods are indispensable to physical life. It has been said about money that you cannot take it with you, but neither can you go anywhere without it. While some values are higher, others are normally prior. Even so, economic values are to be treated as means toward even more important ends.

Progress consists less in plumbing than in personality, even though sanitary plumbing may make some contribution to the preservation of personality. God is concerned that man should have daily bread. Yet it is less of a tragedy to starve for a noble cause than it is to live luxuriously and aimlessly. While our religious tradition is not ascetic in the absolute sense of regarding material goods as evil, it does insist upon an asceticism of proportion that regards the material and the physical as subordinate goods. We are enthusiastically to appreciate the physical, but we are to be rigorous in the consistency and validity of our priorities.

Since economic activity does contribute to such a symmetrical structure of values, participation as a worker in the production of worthwhile products can make an important contribution to personal growth. It becomes an avenue of service and an expression of love. Therefore society needs to make available to all its citizens meaningful work under conditions that contribute to the development of the worker. This means jobs that produce genuine wealth rather than "illth." This means protection against physical hazards, opportunity for satisfying and helpful human relationships, the right to participate in decision-making, positions of dignity and self-respect, and the possibility of creative expression and pride in one's product. Such participation in economic activity becomes a responsible use of freedom in the use of one's life energies.

A second major moral demand is that every man should have equal opportunity for access to available goods. Universalism is to be joined to human fulfillment. Every man deserves a chance for actualization of his potentialities. The genuine needs of men give content to social definitions of rights. Each person has a right to the opportunity to satisfy his needs to the fullest extent possible under the existing outputs of production. Every child should have the maximum possible opportunity to live fully, richly, and harmoniously throughout his life-span. The right to grow and develop the full dimensions of one's humanity is as much a basic human right as is the right to survive. Denial of the possibility of growth is as serious as infanticide. This has important implications for the distribution of the product of the economy. One important way to judge any society is by what happens to the least fortunate or the most disadvantaged group within it.

This is a central economic meaning of the overarching ethical norm of love. Radical good will is an outgoing, active concern without boundaries. When it becomes necessary, it even gives priority to the neighbor, using this term in its most inclusive sense. Kierkegaard insisted that there is one question to which it is impossible to give an incorrect answer. This is the question, "Who is my neighbor?" No matter which person is named, the answer is correct. If one could imagine a telephone directory listing every person in the world, he could put his finger down at random and that person would deserve all the opportunities that culture can provide.

This may well be the place to point out that when we outline general ethical guidelines, we are describing a system that is to be applied as a whole. Given the limitations of nature and of the imperfect human situation, it is scarcely ever possible to realize all values simultaneously. For example, when there is not enough to go around, some discrimination must be shown. To try to keep ten men alive with food sufficient only to sustain five means that all will starve. Ethical norms become goals to be approximated as closely as possible under existing circumstances. In order to do this, one moral claim may need to be subordinated to another in order to preserve the fullest possible realization of the total system of values. The indispensable contribution of ethics to building futures is the pointing of directions, the protesting of inadequacies, and the stimulating of the most expeditious possible movement toward improvement.

A third general observation follows, if one seriously regards human fulfillment of all persons as the test for social activity. This requires more than a serious, but subordinate, emphasis on economic goods and equal opportunity for all persons.

There also needs to be popular control of the process, providing the fullest possible political and economic liberty for all participants. This includes freedom in the negative sense as the absence of coercion. We are not completely free so long as society continues to enforce speed limits, or regulations against the manufacture of impure drugs, or laws against shooting mediocre television producers. Both the sincere conscientious objector and the nonconscientious criminal are subject to the coercion of society. While the restraint of some is necessary to protect the liberty of many, coercion should nevertheless be kept to the minimum necessary to preserve maximum liberty for the total group. This becomes a testimony against aristocracy, tyranny, and totalitarianism. This is a plea for participation in policy decisions, economic as well as political, affecting one's welfare.

Also to be prized is freedom in the positive sense, or the availability of opportunity. A man on a desert island who is an accomplished musician is not completely free. There are no policemen preventing his playing the piano, but there is no piano. It is freedom in this sense which is more extensively discussed later under the heading of equal opportunity. In both the negative and the positive meanings of the term, moral autonomy for the making of choices is necessary to full human growth. Our present society is much better at this point than those which preceded it. But it is not yet good enough. Any new era for man must continue the trend.

A fourth major goal is supportive, dynamic community. This involves the principle of relationship, which recognizes the interdependence of all humankind. Personality cannot be actualized in isolation. A man cannot live as a human being without his neighbor. All that we do affects others and all that others do affects us. The growth of liberty and of equal opportunity depends upon such a sustaining community. Man was created in community, and he finds fulfillment in relationships of love. This includes deeper intimacy in small groups where individuals are reinforced by acceptance and sensitive support.

It also requires more effective participation in the consensus of large groups.

Five principles may be quickly mentioned as guides to relationships that best support personal fulfillment. (1) Supporting communities are more cohesive than divisive, inclusive instead of exclusive. They do not split humanity horizontally into classes or vertically into nations. (2) Such communities need to become more cooperative and less competitive. The common pursuit of similar goals is ethically superior to the antagonistic pursuit of divergent goals. Conflict is necessary and can be creative, but part of its creativity lies in outcomes that make possible greater cooperation. (3) This is related to nonviolence or peace. Harmony, in the deepest sense of the term, is the goal. Destructive conflict, which may even destroy life, is the enemy. Antagonistic force leads to defensive attitudes, resentment, and counterproductive battling. Beating swords into plowshares is a matter not only for international attention but also for policy within a nation. (4) Individual and subgroup interests are to be subordinated to the common good. Whenever these interests cannot be simultaneously realized, what is good for General Motors is less important than what is good for the country. The same thing can be said for labor unions or for individual persons. The fulfillment of persons is the end, but this is contradicted when the growth of one limits the growth of hundreds. (5) To retain any of these desirable characteristics and to remain adequately supportive, groups must dynamically develop, just as individuals grow. Social conditions are never static; social organization must continuously adapt. In times of rapid change, traditional arrangements are more quickly outdated. The resulting tensions tend to shatter supporting groups. The maintenance of community requires continuous change in the patterns of community.

In such an exposition of ethical guidelines, one needs to avoid a simple moralism or naïve idealism. I have already suggested the necessity for making choices within the situation with acute awareness of the total system of values. Furthermore, I do not think of ethical insights as let down by skyhooks in some mysterious revelation that will solve all our problems if given blind obedience. To be sure, there are intuitional elements in ethics, as in science. These include "logically primitive" presuppositions and novel elements in conclusions. The latter involve a "leap of faith" beyond available evidence, but in the direction indicated by the evidence we have. This element of incompletely verified novelty is a part of scientific hypotheses, new industrial processes, and political programs, as well as of ethical recommendations. Apart from these elements, my view of ethics is empirical. Ethical insights grow out of comprehensive experience rationally interpreted, just as do scientific or industrial discoveries. They are likewise validated or modified by further experience. Moral reflection should employ the general features of the scientific method in ways appropriate to subject matter that is more vast and less controllable.

This kind of ethical inquiry the modern man can pursue with enthusiasm. On it he can rely with confidence. This approach to morality takes into account all the relevant political and economic facts and theories and adds to them related data from broader ranges of human experience. Charting policy in accordance with ethical principles then becomes acting with more careful scrutiny and broader perspective than our usual specialized choices. It takes seriously the full range of historical experience, along with more widely inclusive data including ultimate matters. When morality is so defined, it becomes liberating instead of restrictive. An ethical statement is then not so much saying, "Be good," as it is saying, "Don't be stupid." Weakness in ethical sensitivity is simply lack of comprehensive realism. Morality becomes a solid guide for selecting dreams for the future.

It is of major significance then to say that the particular trends toward the future described earlier in this chapter are supported by our highest ethical insight. If one thinks it important to devote economic resources to the end of human fulfillment for all persons, then he will gladly accept acceleration of invention or greater productivity, so long as these are related to constructive outputs. Abundance plus leisure may be used as the foundation for a new quality of freer life stressing higher values. Interdependent contacts with a wider world could make possible new dimensions of supportive, dynamic community.

The relationship between accepted ethical goals and current practices is unfortunately, however, not one of such glorious harmony as this might suggest. Moral considerations also support sharp criticism of some aspects of even the trends we have thus far described. The most helpful ethics always go beyond even the best we have accomplished. Ethical analysis, for example, raises questions about abundance in terms of the kinds of products involved, the justice of their distribution, or possible diminishing returns after some optimum point has been reached. Those questions are not ordinarily raised by short-term self-interest, or tradition, or most authorities with status. Even at our best points, we have not lived well enough by the best we know.

Certainly we have not done so at our worst points. The trends and possibilities thus far described are by no means the only elements in our present situation. Tragic problems have grown out of the same economic and political structures that have provided the notable benefits we have been discussing. To allow such devastating consequences, we have separated ethics from practice in a kind of moral schizophrenia. Or we have rationalized the meaning of our morality in a diligently contrived tangle of logical absurdity. As a consequence of such obscene masquerades of morality, our generation faces quite a different alternative future, which may destroy even the achievements of the past. To this we must now turn.

2
OPTIONS IN FUTURES:
II. Dissonance and Disaster

DESCRIPTIONS OF SOCIAL SYSTEMS easily take on the color of a real estate advertisement. The specifications may sound like the cottage of our dreams, because the termites in the foundations and the truck route in front of the door are not mentioned. Half a description may be accurate as far as it goes, but a general conclusion drawn from it becomes completely inaccurate. It is true that our future may be one of a super-industrial civilization. But this is not the only possibility. There are other trends so ominous that they may lead to a completely different outcome, even to the final elimination of life from this planet. These points of dissonance with our highest ideals may stimulate to improvement. But if dissonance is not deeply enough felt or remains unresolved, it becomes a chronic infection eventually producing convulsions and collapse for civilization.

INEQUALITY WITH EXPECTATIONS OF EQUITY

One serious contradiction of our ideals is the discriminatory nature of our economy. Its full benefits are not shared by all —and this in a day when the poor around the world are more clamorously demanding justice. The distribution of the national product is so unequal as to create the twin monsters of poverty and superfluity. In 1962, the top 5 percent of the United

States population received 20 percent of the national income, while the 20 percent at the bottom received 4.6 percent.[1] Wealth is even less equitably distributed. In 1962, one half of 1 percent of the consumer units (families and independent individuals) owned 22 percent of the country's wealth and 2 percent owned 43 percent, while 95 percent of the less wealthy owned another 43 percent and 26 percent owned less than one half of 1 percent.[2] To restate these statistical data in graphic representation of the distribution of wealth: America's dinner table is so arranged that at one end one person reaches out to something over ten plates, the next two people may eat from approximately four plates, the next eight from five, while finally nine chairs are clustered around half a plate. What would be the interpersonal relationships within a family if dinners were divided in that way? We want our national life to reflect something of the qualities of a family, with common goals, low crime rates, and full cooperation. Yet we are unwilling to admit and to remove one of the basic causes of tension and turmoil among us.

We repress statistics more easily because we have made poverty ecologically invisible by confining it in ghettos hidden from the freeways. It is culturally hidden because in an urban situation we judge people by their immediate outward appearance. In this respect our clothes and cars can look pretty much alike. Psychologically we blot out the facts about poverty because they are too painful to acknowledge. How can you think about standards of living in Appalachia or Africa while eating a steak dinner? Ethically the impact of poverty is often eliminated because of our loss of sensitivity and empathy. This is hardness of heart, in Scriptural terms. One of the most destructive epidemic diseases is the mass amnesia of the suburb. Bishop Gore needs to be quoted more often: "Love is the capacity to read statistics with compassion."

The blight of poverty on personality is intensified by poor housing, crowding, less education, undeveloped capacities, strains on the family, and generally limited opportunities. Poverty is associated with disease, dependency, and delinquency. Inability to control one's destiny contributes to frustration and anxiety. The costs of serious inequality include divisions in community, and the resentment and rebellion of a revolutionary situation.

While many are poor, the wealthy are still given status and disproportionate influence among us. For a large portion of the population, Hugh Hefner's reputation is enhanced by the report of his five-and-a-half-million-dollar, jet-black super-DC9 with elliptical bed covered with Tasmanian opossum and motorized swivel chair upholstered in Himalayan goatskin.[3] Aristotle Onassis and Jacqueline Kennedy are reported to have spent, during their first year of marriage, five million dollars for jewelry and other gifts to Mrs. Onassis, one and two tenths million for her personal expenses and a comparable amount for maintaining the luxury yacht *Christina*, and expenses for 202 servants and bodyguards.[4]

The value system held by our society becomes the more disgraceful when we enlarge perspectives to include other nations of the world. Robert L. Heilbroner has outlined the changes that would follow if an American suburban family was transformed into a typical family in the undeveloped world. First their house is stripped of its furniture—everything except a few frayed blankets, one chair, and a kitchen table. All clothes disappear, except that each member of the family wears his oldest suit or dress, a shirt or blouse. The head of the family may keep a pair of shoes, but the others must do without. Along with the kitchen appliances go the contents of the cupboards, except for a box of matches, a small bag of flour, a bit of sugar and salt, some moldy potatoes, a few onions, and a dish of dried beans. Next all utilities are shut off—gas, electricity, running water. Then the house itself is taken away and the family moves to the tool shed. Newspapers, magazines, books, television are gone. One radio might remain, though this raises the family above the typical. Social services are discontinued. There is no longer a postman or a fireman. The two-classroom school is three miles away, and the midwife-operated clinic is ten miles distant. The family may keep five dollars, but any regular replenishing of that hoard is doubtful.[5]

For two thirds of the world's population the major nutritional problem is malnutrition. Our number-one nutritional problem is obesity. An appropriate amendment to the Lord's Prayer might be, "Forgive us this day our daily bread." The call to repentance is particularly strong since our standard of living partly depends upon exploitation of the mines and plantations of the Third World, on their low wages, and on low selling prices for their products. The United States, with about 6 percent of the world's population, consumes about 40 percent of the world's production of natural resources. On what possible basis can we defend the consumption of so much by so few? Yet when someone suggests a modest increase in the part of our wealth invested in technical assistance or capital transference, or a modification of trade policies in favor of developing nations, there is a great outcry—the familiar reaction of the rich before the deluge that sweeps them away. Three continents (Asia, Africa, and South America) are in revolt against inferiority, exploitation, and inequality. The failure of the United States to understand and support such aspirations may prove to be our greatest policy blunder during this century.

Inequality also has more immediate consequences for the privileged. It encourages the idolatry of materialism, making it easy to evaluate too highly that to which they cling. Success easily leads to pride and self-satisfaction. Those who are more fortunate may think too highly of themselves, concluding that "my power and the might of my hand have gotten me this wealth" (Deut. 8:17). Such contentment easily becomes unwarranted conservatism and moral blindness. The decline of compassion solidifies into neglect of neighbor as a way of life. Selfishness and exploitation are all too easily rationalized. At the same time they contribute to alienation and isolation from the majority of our fellow creatures. As Saul Alinsky suggested, the poor cannot eat and the rich cannot sleep—for fear that the poor will plunder their wealth. For all these reasons, wealthy estates may constitute an undesirable neighborhood. Upper-class children are also culturally disadvantaged, and the United States is a morally undeveloped country.[6]

There is considerable evidence that our public policy is helping the rich grow richer and penalizing the poor by higher tax rates. Many taxes, especially sales and property taxes, are regressive in effect. That is, they take a larger proportion of the poor person's income than of the rich man's, since the poor person spends a higher percentage of his total income on taxable items. For example, a study of the impact of the property tax in California showed an exceedingly regressive pattern, the amount paid ranging from 9 percent of the income of those with family incomes of $2,000, to 3 percent paid by those with incomes of $20,000.[7] Furthermore, the federal income tax is much less progressive than we imagine. Loopholes allow actual tax payments by high income groups to level off instead of continuing the increasing rates provided for in progressive tables. Joseph W. Barr, former undersecretary of the Treasury, cites the extreme cases in 1967 of 21 persons with incomes over $1,000,000 who paid no federal income taxes at all.[8] In addition, federal social security taxes are regressive and tend to erase part of the mildly progressive effect of the income tax.

The combined result is that in 1965 the one third of United States families receiving the least income paid 30 percent of their income in federal, state, and local taxes. The one third in the middle-income range paid 26 percent, and the one third receiving the highest incomes paid 33 percent. At the very bottom of the lower third, those with incomes under $2,000 paid 44 percent of income in taxes.[9] At the same time those with incomes of $15,000 and over paid only 38 percent.[10] So far as taxation policy goes, we reverse Robin Hood by taking from the poor and favoring the rich.

There are substitute welfare payments made by government to the poor that appear to relieve the regressive features of taxation. On the other hand, there are also various kinds of government aid to business. Subsidies and allowances are made to the oil industry, aerospace or defense firms, and large farmers, among others. We have often given low-interest housing loans to the middle class more readily than rent subsidies to the poor, or we have built freeways for suburban car-owners before rapid transit for the inner-city poor.

Fortunately tax reform is very much in the air these days. State and local governments could rely more heavily on income taxes and less on sales and property taxes. The federal government might alleviate the payroll tax to the poor, close loopholes in income tax, make estate and gift taxes more effective, and establish more steeply graduated rates. Joseph Pechman, the director of economic studies at Brookings Institute, spoke of possible future changes but concluded, "In the meantime, the tax system will continue to disgrace the most affluent nation in the world." [11]

Ethics, with regard to poverty and inequality, does not support a demand for completely equal wealth or income. As a matter of fact, such equality would deny the basic principle of equal opportunity. Each man has somewhat different needs. Giving a family that has had costly illness the same amount as others receive is actually to provide them with less opportunity. Anatole France long ago lamented that the law in its majestic impartiality forbids rich and poor alike to sleep under bridges and to steal bread. The central point is that any pattern of distribution is to be evaluated in terms of the purpose of consumption, which is the fulfillment of persons. Every man has a right to the same access to such fulfillment, to make the most possible of whatever capacities he has. This will require some inequality of income. But it will not justify the degree of inequality now existing.

Several arguments have been used in defense of greater inequalities. For one thing, it is said that the expenditures of the rich keep industry prosperous and provide jobs for workers. This overlooks the fact that manufacturing for the needs of the poor would provide the same prosperity and jobs. The same argument for supporting prosperity could be made for the criminal class, since without them policemen and prison guards would be thrown out of work. Vandalism and arson make work for carpenters, and war should then be welcomed as one of the most effective stimulators of industry and employment.

A second argument is that we ought not to kill the goose that lays the golden egg. Vast wealth is necessary to sustain philanthropy—unless, of course, we substitute many small gifts. Admittedly this would pose some difficulty, since lower income people feel a greater urgency about using their money for their own immediate needs. Yet why should one have a greater right to allocate charitable contributions than do others? Many persons would like to give large sums to the causes they consider good. Such democratization of philanthropy would seem quite appropriate in a free society.

It is easy for the holder of wealth to slip into the assumption that somehow he deserves it. This is particularly horrifying in the case of inherited wealth, when the only action of the holder was a wise choice of grandparents! Frank H. Knight has gone further to ask why an individual should be entitled to earnings because of inherited personal capacity any more than because of inherited property.[12] Nor can anyone claim superior merit when society has added prejudice to poverty, disqualifying the poor and the black from the competition. The rich may well have worked hard, but what of the desperate labor of those trying to maintain a family on a pittance?

Nor can we relieve guilt by arguing that the poor are to blame for their own plight. An occasional few are. Poverty, however, is concentrated in our country among the old, broken families with female heads, the racial minorities, and the poorly educated—circumstances generally beyond the control of the victim. Insofar as some are poor because society has not supplied enough jobs to go around, "welfare reform" should begin with full employment measures. Insofar as the poor are the products of a culture of poverty that resists their rising above it, it is folly to continue the policies that perpetuate the vicious circle instead of admitting that the able-bodied poor have the same capacities as others and will show these if given opportunity. By perpetuating the poverty–low education–poverty cycle we plow under generation after generation of brains among the poor.

Some justify concentrations of wealth as economic necessity. It is argued that capital accumulation is essential for the benefits of industrialization, and so long as we have a private property system someone must hold the title deeds. This argument begs the question. It offers no reason for concentration of ownership instead of wider dispersal, and it still leaves the question of what is to be done with the income derived from the title. Whatever may be said about lesser degrees of inequality, there is no convincing argument in defense of continued differences of the dimensions now existing. This is immorality of a magnitude seldom before practiced in history.

Speaking theologically, present inequality violates the universal intention of God. In desiring full opportunity for personal fulfillment, God does not play favorites. The prophetic word is not parochial. God causes his rain to fall on the just and on the unjust (Matt. 5:45). Amos represents God as saying to those who consider themselves a chosen people, "Are you not like the Ethiopians to me?" (Amos 9:7). The provision of opportunity is a major expression of love directed toward the full actualization of every person. As indicated in the parables of the laborers in the vineyard and the prodigal son, radical love goes beyond the requirements of formal justice. The needs of others define the duties of the self. The message of the parable of the good Samaritan is that needs anywhere constitute a claim on resources everywhere. "If any one has the world's goods and sees his brother in need, yet closes his heart against him, how does God's love abide in him?" (I John 3:17; see also James 2:15–17.)

Such an ethic of outgoing concern impels one in a special way to stand beside the poor. As Karl Barth put it for the church: "Casting all false impartiality aside, the Church must concentrate first on the lower and lowest levels of human society. The poor, the socially and economically weak and threatened, will always be the object of its primary and particular concern." [13] The Judeo-Christian faith is one of liberation. Any social arrangement that perpetuates human subordination or bondage no longer carries the impulse of Exodus or Easter.

Reinhold Niebuhr emphasized that in the Bible "specially severe judgments fall upon the rich and the powerful." [14] Amos spoke woe "to those who lie upon beds of ivory" and "trample upon the poor." He insisted that God would not listen to the worship of those who denied justice. (Amos 6:4, 5:11–24; see also Isa. 5:8–10, 58:3–12.) The more we have, the more is expected of us (Luke 12:48). In the Bible, sharing is "a duty of justice, not an optional generosity." [15] Wherever there is a poor man, the Old Testament injunction is, "You shall open wide your hand to your brother" (Deut. 15:7–11). The New Testament word is that where love is genuine, "Your abundance at the present time should supply their want, so that their abundance may supply your want, that there may be equality" (II Cor. 8:8–14). The rich and the powerful are often reluctant gatekeepers to opportunity. Because of the perils of privilege Jesus said, "It is easier for a camel to go through the eye of a needle than for a rich man to enter the kingdom of God" (Matt. 19:24).

In view of the world position of the United States today, probably the major ethical problem of our nation is how a rich man can be saved. By continuing our commonly accepted standard of living, we are denying life to others. What is the difference between shooting a man and starving him to death? When world famine develops within a few years, the guilt of maintaining our comforts will be greater than when we dropped the first atomic bomb.

In Christian history, charity has been the most commonly recommended solution for the problem of economic inequality.[16] Now we have learned that even this is not enough. Giving by the rich to the poor inevitably involves paternalism, which is a denial of liberty. This is clear when "strings are attached" to the gift. Even without such conditions it is inherently true, since the gift always depends on the unilateral decision of him who has the excess resources. Theological insight into the nature of man should allow us to see that if one has power and the other has not, the chances are that the first will not do all that he ought to do.

Ethical sensitivity does not require equality in economic distribution, but it does call for considerably less inequality than we now have. We need to be shocked into serious recognition of the deep dissonance between our accepted ideal and our actual practice at this point, just as we were a few years ago in the field of race relations. Which is the more obscene, a nude woman or one bountifully draped in furs and jewels while millions slowly starve? If we prosecute those who incite to local riot, how can we excuse those whose policies lead to desperation and violence in the Third World?

Waste While Resources Dwindle

To turn to another major point of dissonance, our society is characterized not only by marvels of technological achievements but also by such conspicuous waste as to become a self-destructive society. A wide miscellany of wasteful practices can be quickly enumerated. We suffer from duplication of services (which result, for example, when an Eastern manufacturer sends his product West and a Western competitor ships essentially the same product East), misuse of factors of production in manufacturing useless or harmful goods, the restrictive practices of monopoly (whether in the enforcement of scarcity or withholding inventions by big business or in the "featherbedding" requirements of labor unions), and the idleness of factors of production (either chronically or during depressions). It has been estimated that about 30 percent of the men in developing countries are permanently unemployed, and that during the great depression of the thirties, by using the idle factors of production, we could have replaced all the reproducible assets in the country.[17] The progress of our economy has moved something like the politician's waltz, two steps forward and one step back!

With respect to exhaustion of natural resources, one of our more serious practices is "death-dating," or planned obsolescence. This is manipulation of quality to fix an early time for the product to wear out. This reduction of durability creates a junkman's paradise. It also has a psychological version causing products to wear out in the owner's mind, since he is under pressure to conform to regular style changes. A woman becomes unhappy with a closet full of good-as-new dresses, while her husband overestimates his need for a new-model car. The shoddy workmanship of planned obsolescence is also an affront to the worker who has a sense of vocation. Insofar as it uselessly dissipates natural resources it is rebellion against a creator God.

We may become more sensitive to this because of the awakening interest in the problem of environmental pollution. Expanded production has also created massive filth. *Time* magazine recently summarized: "Every year, Americans junk seven million cars, 100 million tires, 20 million tons of paper, 28 billion bottles and 48 billion cans. . . . The U.S. also produces almost 50% of the world's industrial pollution." We turn oceans into rubbish dumps and create a gigantic "sewer in the sky." [18] We are exceeding the capacities of rivers and lakes to absorb our wastes, and the future may bring death to the world's oceans. Especially when current processes are combined with continuing population growth, man's survival is at stake.[19] Unless we solve these problems, we are told that man's life expectancy on earth may be only a few hundred years instead of what could otherwise be hundreds of millions of years.

While this book concentrates on domestic problems, international wars must be mentioned as one of the most disastrous wastes faced by all the nations in the world. As Senator Fulbright has put it, "Violence is our most important product." [20] About sixty cents out of each federal tax dollar is used to pay for wars—past, present, and future. Yet the world is less secure because of the terror of modern weaponry. This is a dismal economic disaster because it diverts to death the energies and resources desperately needed for new life, through relieving poverty, rebuilding cities, rescuing the environment, or helping developing nations become economically self-generating. In speaking of the Mekong Delta project with its amazing potential for food for southeast Asia, Lester B. Pearson wrote, "It would make the angels weep to think that less than one third of the money that has been spent in one year by the United States in the prosecution of the Vietnam war would complete this wonderfully imaginative project." [21]

This becomes the more serious in an inclusive or theological perspective. The Biblical view is that man is to cooperate with nature to fulfill the purposes of God. Hebrew law, prophetic utterance, and the teachings of Jesus make it clear that material things are to be managed to contribute to human need. This includes a consideration not only of all men now on earth but also of all generations yet to come. Ecological realities impose limits on the indefinite increase of material production. We have no alternative other than to respect the natural or ecological limits of the material universe. We are learning that this means reducing personal demands for the sake of others, keeping standards of living as well as size of populations within bounds. We are not to neglect or exploit nature, but to cherish and cooperate with nature to fulfill its grand design.

REPRESSION IN AN AGE OF LIBERATION

Our politico-economic practices not only continue to be discriminatory, unequal, regressive, and wasteful. They are also in important respects manipulative and freedom-denying. As a result, instead of universal participation in one man–one vote decisions, there are disproportionate concentrations of power. This, too, may prove disastrous in a day when the revolutionary expectations of restless mankind include equal participation in formulating social policy.

Economic inequality in itself means that some make more socially consequential decisions than others. Edmund A. Opitz denies this by arguing: "If a man uses the piece of earth that is his to build a house on, and plants it with grass, wheat, potatoes, and if he lives peacefully in his own home and reaps the harvest he has sown, he is a free man. He is not coercing anyone." [22] If this man owns a vast estate and half the potato fields in the state, it is hard to accept the conclusion that his freedom is completely shared by others. Even if he owns only a tiny plot and someone wants to cut across it to the next street, he exercises some control over the pedestrian. What is exercise of freedom to one man is coercion to another. As the property controlled by one man increases, the number of ways in which he limits the action of others becomes more extensive. A theological view of man helps us to understand how easily the bias of narrow individual or group interest enters into such controlling decisions. Part of the message of high religion is that we are never as objective or permissive as we think we are.

Advertising is a major illustration of the engineering of consent. In forming American life-styles it competes effectively with churches and schools, and expands its influence from the economic into the political sphere. Governors and presidents are now sold to the public by the same techniques used for deodorants and dog food. In both cases those who can afford the cost of the campaign have the advantage.

An ethical evaluation of advertising is not a simple matter. Not every attempt at influencing opinion is to be considered nefarious. Advertising can perform an important educational function, informing the public about new products or discount sales. Advertising can usefully promote a United Fund campaign or a needed social reform. Advertising has made possible the mass markets that allow mass production and lower prices.

Such benefits must be weighed against serious abuses. Duplicity or contrived superficiality is far from any criteria of sincerity or truth-telling. Much advertising distracts the customer from the most relevant questions. No auto manufacturer would dream of buying his steel on the basis of a double-page advertisement in a periodical. Yet he expects consumers to buy cars on that basis. Or, even when the content is acceptable, the method is psychologically manipulative. Such violations of individual autonomy depend upon keeping an audience in a passive, receptive mood with its critical faculties at least partially paralyzed.

Advertising has often been not only misleading and manipulative, but also materialistic and monopolistic. When advertising is paid for by those who want to sell goods, it is understandable that it should popularize a material standard of living. The primary measure of a man's worth is made to appear as the quantity of products consumed, the comforts of his home, or the appeal of his sexuality. This involves seduction in the sense of triggering lower, short-run, and selfish motivations to induce a person to do what he would not do if he acted according to his highest, long-run, and altruistic values. This encourages waste and distorts the economy toward a pattern of production emphasizing advertised goods instead of our chief needs. All this is corrosive to the national character. As physical scientists must decide whether or not to use their talents in research for more destructive bombs, so social scientists must choose whether to lend their talents to the preparation of this kind of advertising.

The monopolistic threat of advertising arises because it is coupled with so great a concentration of economic power. This is obvious in industries in which price or quality competition has nearly vanished. Even short of such oligopoly of a few large producers, the general point of view publicized by industry is often not matched by equally powerful economic interests speaking for consumers or the poor. Demand can then be managed by the seller. This raises the basic question of who ought to control the economy. As was indicated earlier, economic activity has ethical significance at two points, in providing products contributing to the fulfillment of consumers and in making possible meaningful and creative use of the life energy of workers. Both of these outcomes depend on the consumer being accepted as the person for whom all the wheels go round. This is obviously true of the first function. It is also true of the second, because the definition of meaningful output must be written in terms of service to consumers. While other associations exist to protect the more limited interests of workers of all kinds (including managers and professional people), there is a strong case for consumer control of the goals toward which economic activity is directed. (Since everyone is a consumer, some would prefer to say "citizen control," but this raises issues that will be discussed later.) There is widespread agreement among economists of all shades of opinion that consumers should perform this general function.

The traditional capitalist theory about it was that King Consumer caused all manufacturers and suppliers to do obeisance to him because of the allocation of his purchasing power. The choices of consumers were thought of as a continuous referendum. There is obviously some kind of referendum going on, since producers cannot sell unless consumers buy. The question is whether consumers have an opportunity to buy what they want or whether, as in a political plebiscite in a dictatorship, they have the opportunity of voting "yes" or "yes." Unfortunately, there are extremely significant differences between a purchasing power referendum and effective participation in one man–one vote decision-making. For one thing, consumers as voters cannot choose the candidates. They are nominated by the producers. For example, consumers cannot vote for items they would like to have produced with a subsidy, with losses covered by profits from other items. Neither can the consumer effectively propose that instead of many different models of a product, he would prefer a single standard model, which could then be made at a lower price. He is helpless to allocate purchasing power toward such a model until some manufacturer chooses to make it. Furthermore, consumers cannot initiate or participate in an effective campaign prior to the voting. All the effective speaking is done in one direction, directed at the consumers from the advertisers. Or again, not all men have equal votes in this curious referendum. The wants of the rich are overrepresented by plural voting. For all these reasons it can be said that the consumer does not have the direct, effective ballot which is necessary for control. He is controlled instead of controlling. Consumers also have cause to demand participatory democracy.

Beyond the problem faced by consumers, the growth of large business units, not answerable to the people as a whole, can threaten other freedoms also. Huge corporations, labor unions, trade associations, or professional groups can become centers of entrenched power. For example, "shareholders democracy" does not effectively exist in a large corporation where ownership is separated from control. Stock is too widely scattered, and there is no way of debating the issues. Most additional capital may be generated within the corporation from reinvested profits, and therefore there is no dependence on attracting new investors. The military-industrial complex illustrates the problem in comparatively unchecked power. Individuals become lost in this kind of mass. This organizational pattern easily becomes an instrument for repression.

Because he believes that the critical faculties of the people have been suffocated by indoctrination and manipulation, Herbert Marcuse concludes, "Democracy would appear to be the most efficient system of domination." [23] This statement unduly minimizes approaches to power still open to the people, but it recognizes resistances to democracy that may yet be our undoing. Scholars disagree about the extent of concentration of social control, but there is no disagreement about the fact that the economically powerful have disproportionate influence in other social institutions.[24] Typically, the economically powerful elite is treated with deference and given a larger voice on the boards of social service agencies, or in determining educational policy, and even in ecclesiastical organizations. There are serious implications for democracy when economic power becomes disproportionately effective in politics. There has frequently been unequal treatment in the courts, legislatures, and executive decisions. The whispers of a few constituents often mean more in the ear of a public official than the shouts of hundreds of the less economically prestigious. Fortunately there have been differences of opinion within the elite, but even so, in both domestic and foreign policy, democracy has been severely strained by the weight given to economic leadership.

Concentrations of economic power can become particularly dangerous now that the mass media have become both more effective and more expensive. Those with superior financial resources can afford to buy more time. They are also those who have been well treated by existing economic arrangements. Why should they want to change them? This kind of conservative bias more easily appears not only in the commercials but in the general character of programming. For example, since huge audiences must be maintained, innocuous entertainment is more likely to be sponsored than divisive presentations of controversial matters. But democracy requires controversy to bring issues to the attention of the people who are not Ph.D.'s, or who do not read heavy books. In our system they too are expected to have an opinion. Freedom of the press is a basic democratic necessity, but unfortunately it does not carry with it the capital to operate a press. Neither does freedom of assembly or of speech come completely equipped with meeting halls and a radio network. Under these circumstances some are more free than others.

Ethical analysis has repeatedly raised the question of the relationship of power concentrations to social justice. Man's inclination to injustice and self-interest makes power inequalities dangerous, particularly when power is tied to the search for private profit. Under these circumstances the social situation becomes easily defined through the expression of self-interest of the stronger. Justice is more likely to be achieved under a dispersal of power where those who have less immediate interest can contribute greater objectivity and where those who have contrary interests may also be a balancing part of the debate.

To a considerable extent ours is a traditional society, ill equipped to deal with accelerating change and "future shock." Man's typical reluctance to alter his habits has been reinforced by the groups that have easiest access to our abundant means for manufacturing consent. We live in a basically revolutionary situation. If we do not rapidly find new ways for giving effective votes to the dispossessed, valued institutions will be unnecessarily swept away in mankind's insistence on liberation.

MISMANAGED PRIORITIES
WHEN OLD VALUES DEPRECIATE

Now, during one of the greatest transition periods of all history, when we need to move on to a new preoccupation, our very success in technological production has bred an attachment to the material things to which we devoted our greatest past energy. Our primary orientation is still too largely materialistic. Men to a great extent have become mechanized extensions of machines designed to produce material products. Pius XI said as far back as *Quadragesimo anno* (1931), "Dead matter leaves the factory ennobled and transformed, where men are corrupted and degraded." In an exaggerated emphasis on technology and material consumption, man loses touch with himself and leaves undeveloped the higher potentialities of his nature. So to set things above men is a dangerous form of idolatry.

With all of his social developments man has also drifted into unnecessary bondage to his material environment. We say that we "cannot live" without extra telephone extensions, air-conditioned cars, or electric carving knives. Even economists are beginning to recognize that further increase in quantity of goods for the affluent may destroy the possibility of an improved quality of life. Galbraith in his quotable style has said: "To furnish a barren room is one thing. To continue to crowd in furniture until the foundation buckles is quite another." [25] "Overfeed" capacity in economics is as dangerous as "overkill" capacity in international affairs, when it pollutes the environment, increases world inequality, and wastes resources. If even the present population of the rest of the world should achieve the current United States standard of living, there would not be enough copper, tin, and lead left in the world to permit this on the basis of known technology. How can we then justify motors to reduce muscular strain in rolling up car windows and at the same time mechanical contrivances in neighborhood gyms to increase muscular exertion?

Any enlightened system of ethics would seriously question the mass hedonism of our times, with happiness defined largely as unlimited consumption. Character is corroded by luxury, and concentration on lower values produces personal deterioration. Selfish enjoyment of that kind of abundance brings boredom, frustration, and meaninglessness. Leisure uninvested in creativity becomes torment. Heavy concentration on physical values passes a point of diminishing returns. The question must eventually be faced: What will you do for an encore? Such limited awareness does not expect enough of life. It is the opposite of a full, authentic life, intensification of experience, and release of undisclosed possibilities in a new man.

Instead of shifting private and government expenditures toward a new quality of culture, we continue to pour wealth into expanded gadgetry. In August, 1971, President Nixon announced a reversal of economic policy to include wage and price controls in dealing with inflation and recession. Although the new policy had its merits, he was still acting on the basis of outdated assumptions at the point here being discussed. His program anticipated that by lowering taxes and encouraging business, consumers would continue to buy increased amounts of the kinds of things private industry is equipped to produce. In a really new game plan, in which we seriously intend to reduce gadgets and increase services to meet unmet needs, we may need to raise taxes and then to stimulate prosperity and employment through government investment in schools, low-cost housing, VISTA programs, or a different type of production. At the same time, a shift in priorities would result in greatly reduced government expenditures at other points. Yet taxpayers in the middle and upper brackets, if they are genuinely concerned about poverty and the full range of human need, will be willing and even eager to pay more taxes for such humanitarian purposes.

There are deep contradictions in the possibilities for our economic future. On the one hand we can move toward the kind of new civilization described in the first chapter. There are trends in that direction. But there are also deeply ingrained resistances and powerful countertrends. As the Old Testament prophets dramatically pointed out, continuation of immorality is followed by doom. "Woe to those who call evil good and good evil, who put darkness for light and light for darkness. . . . As the tongue of fire devours the stubble, and as dry grass sinks down in the flame, so their root will be as rottenness, and their blossom go up like dust." (Isa. 5:20, 24.) Our present economy cannot continue its immoral perpetuation of poverty, or war, or pollution, or waste without such catastrophe as the world has never experienced. If rich countries continue their present policy toward poor countries, their children will be swallowed up in the rebellion of the hungry masses of Asia, Africa, and Latin America. If we continue to profit out of present inequalities, and if we neglect rebuilding our cities for people to live in, the disorder and the crime and the revolt of the alienated will put us all back into an overpopulated stone age with skyscraper caves. If the so-called "leading" nations do not stop developing and stockpiling more devastating weapons, we may not make it around the corner into the twenty-first century. As long as by our niggardliness we rob our children of high-quality education, we are participating in one of the worst forms of grand larceny, with a consequent penalty that would make a prison term mild by comparison. The words of Thomas Jefferson are required reading: "I tremble for my country when I reflect that God is just."

We need an earthquake in values comparable to the scientific and technological changes we are experiencing. We now need to "transcend MIT" and General Motors, and perhaps even the Roman Catholic Church or the moderate liberals in the National Council of Churches. Ours is a self-indulgent society, oriented to personal satisfaction more than to social creativity. Our culture too much embodies affluence without altruism and technology without transcendent reference. We are specialists without purpose and sensualists without heart. Until we feel this dissonance powerfully enough, there is little chance for improvement. So long as the unresolved inconsistencies continue, we remain inept to such an extent that our left hand never knows what our left hand is doing and we specialize in wringing defeat out of the very jaws of victory.

Attempts to "strengthen the moral fiber of youth" or "restore loyalty to traditional virtues" are doomed to failure because socially sanctioned, popularly accepted group values are in themselves wrong. So long as each generation continues to be so indoctrinated, this will only intensify the crisis of our times. As it was in Jesus' day, the chief problem is not the defectives or criminals among us, serious as that is, but the "normal" members of society who have status in the community and in the church. The time has come to speak with all seriousness about our common failings. Until we do so, even an idealistic people can continue to sponsor starvation in the midst of potential plenty and drift to war in a world longing for peace.

3
RESTRUCTURING
THE FOUNDATIONS

THE FUTURE DIRECTION for civilization will not be determined simply by deliberation in a professor's study or prayers at the altar or hearings before legislative committees, important as all these are. The forces to be tamed and directed include the vast resources of entire economic systems and the full power of entire nations. The outcome will emerge from a clash between major competing systems from various modifications of capitalism, through mixed economies and mild forms of socialism, to more thoroughgoing and totalitarian planned economies. Each of these has its body of adherents with missionary zeal to achieve world dominance. Each has developed what it considers to be a coherent economic theory supported by an accumulation of capital and wealth invested in a going concern. Each is backed by vast propaganda machines and armies. The outcome of the conflict between them will determine our economic and political future. Professorial study, pastoral prayers, and legislative hearings, to be at all pertinent to our major social decisions, must be somehow related to this clash of competing systems. This chapter will concentrate on such an exploration of basic economic structures, with later reference also to related political aspects.

Any adequate analysis requires the marriage of macroeconomics and macroethics. Macroeconomics involves a model of total economy and a study of its major structures and processes, as over against the investigation of a particular tariff rate or business decision. As Kenneth Boulding said of the economic system of John Maynard Keynes, "It is bulldozer economics, designed to push large problems around, not scalpel economics designed for fine operations." [1] The study of basic systems also calls for macroethics, or the relating of general norms to entire institutions. This is in contrast with microethics, or the exploration of detailed choices within a system. Ethicists can play "gold teeth games" within a Nazi concentration camp, or they can analyze totalitarianism as a major political option. A sound society requires discussion of the morality of beating slaves, but also of the entire system of slavery.

The Appearance of Our Inheritance

Mankind has lived, and either suffered or prospered, under several major economic systems. Since classical times these have included slavery, where men were owned as the basic means of production, and feudalism, with its land-based hierarchy of responsibility and allegiance. Our recent history most significantly begins with the rise of capitalism at the time of the Industrial Revolution. While the original capitalist model has been modified almost beyond recognition, many of its features together with its underlying theory are still very much alive and affecting current decisions in Congress, in the United States Chamber of Commerce, and in the AFL-CIO. The characteristic features of the capitalist system raise ethical and economic issues that must be faced before any mature economic choice can be made by modern man.

Inventions like the flying shuttle and the spinning jenny and the steam engine accelerated the development of a new economic structure. Regardless of how one may wish to evaluate capitalism today, in its beginnings this was a major progressive change that made possible the economic achievements of the past century and laid the foundations for a possible super-industrial society in the future. It was also associated with the development of modern democracy, bringing expanding enfranchisement to previously neglected sectors of the population.

The dominance of capitalism in the Western world was preceded by a major religious change, the Protestant Reformation. One of the most intriguing theories in the social sciences is that which holds that this religious change was an indispensable causal element without which the contribution of capitalism could not have been made. This relationship was explored particularly by Max Weber in a series of monumental studies, part of which have been translated as *The Protestant Ethic and the Spirit of Capitalism*.[2]

In spite of his detractors, Weber made a strong case for the influence of basic theological positions, such as the doctrine of the calling, on decisive social transitions. This strengthens the proposition that there is a self-generating quality about religion that gives it an autonomous influence in the affairs of man. As one economist has put it, "Of all the elements of culture which shape economic institutions, religious practices particularly play a key role—a doubly important one because many other elements of the pattern of life . . . are themselves profoundly affected by the prevailing religious beliefs." [3]

Capitalism, however, claimed its own autonomy and provided a basic social philosophy that did not always accord with the highest insights of religion. This philosophy included some universal generalizations about man as egoistic, rationalistic, and individualistic, which were thought to have been scientifically discovered in nature. Since uncoerced man could be depended upon to act rationally to maximize his individual gratifications, it was thought possible to set up an automatic, self-regulating mechanism to manage economic affairs. Such free acts were also expected to result in the common good through the automatic adjustments of the market.

As a multitude of independent decisions impinged upon each other, a multiplication of beautiful and harmonious outcomes was to be anticipated.[4] Such a system was expected to supply the best allocation of resources to satisfy human wants. If consumers did not want what was being produced, demand and prices would go down, and capital would shift out of that type of production into another line. If consumers wanted more than was being produced, the price of that product would go up and capital would be attracted. Likewise the labor force was expected to be allocated as wages went up in areas of scarcity and down in situations of oversupply. A similar allocation might be made between present needs and investment for the future by fluctuations in interest rates. It was also expected that the devices of the market would stimulate improvement and more efficient production. Since no one producer could raise price unilaterally, he could get more for himself only by reducing his costs. Others would then have to imitate his superior practices or go out of business.

All these automatic adjustments presupposed private entrepreneurs seeking maximum profit in competition with others. Everyone was expected to act acquisitively and competitively. The automatic operation of the market depended upon it. Given such responses, the economic process was thought to be self-regulating, with no danger of exploitation. Power was seen as dispersed and checked by the egoism of others. If a producer charged too high a price, he would be deserted by his customers. If an employer paid too low a wage, he would be deserted by his workers. Outside intervention was seen as destroying the value of the system by destroying incentive, penalizing the competent, or undermining automatic controls.

The structures that grew out of this formidable theory of classical capitalism had three basic characteristics: private ownership of the means of production, the acquisitive motive, and free competition.

The theory of beneficent outcomes of this system depended upon an economic structure composed of many independent buyers and sellers, none large enough to influence price. There was nothing in these basic characteristics, however, to prevent success in competition from producing business units of such size as to violate this essential condition of a free market. As

Finer points out, concentration of control in large corporations "is the simple, natural product of the acquisitive man in a system of competition." [5] Tremendous additional pressures toward bigness are now being exerted by modern technological requirements, such as the multiplication of specialized personnel, the accumulation of unprecedented amounts of capital, or the costliness of research and invention. Efficient mass production is possible only for a large corporation. Some of them have become gigantic.

In 1969 the fifty largest manufacturing corporations held 38 percent of all assets used in manufacturing. The five hundred largest corporations had 74 percent. The five manufacturing corporations employing the most people, hired 11 percent of the total working force engaged in manufacturing. In 1968 the gross revenues of General Motors were more than three times the total revenue of the State of New York and about one eighth of the receipts of the United States government. [6] The turnover of General Motors has been calculated as exceeding the gross national product of Belgium or Switzerland, while the sales of Standard Oil (New Jersey) are reported to exceed the gross national product of Denmark or Austria or Turkey or a considerable number of smaller states. [7] If the largest 150 firms (of the total twelve million American enterprises) were eliminated, Heilbroner calculates that "the nation would come to a standstill." Manufacturing and distribution would collapse. Cities would starve. The majority of families would be bankrupted. [8]

Huge conglomerates combine many different kinds of production, including in one single corporation electrical equipment, life insurance, houses, car rentals, hotels, bakery products, and other assorted items. These giants of the business world are also increasingly striding across national boundaries, becoming multinational. In commenting on Arnold Toynbee's suggestion that such multinational giants might locate their headquarters on some attractive, independent island that "might be persuaded to lend itself as a kind of Vatican City as a seat for the world's multinational corporations," U.S. News & World Re-

port commented: "In such a setting, corporate managers could direct their huge firms without interference from even the largest governments. And their influence on all corners of the world would rival that of political leaders." [9]

The mixed consequences of the new way of doing things include some desirable outcomes. Size may allow greater efficiency of operation, the benefits of which may be at least partially shared with consumers. Costs may be lowered by economies in purchasing and distribution, more productive machinery, or mass markets. Superior products may result from the ability to do more research and adopt more innovations. Large corporations may minimize risks, improve coordination, balance savings and investment, provide capital, and control supply and demand. Size, however, does not always lower costs. Possible benefits may be at least partially balanced by the appearance of bureaucracy and the wastes associated with it. When corporations become larger than a number of the world's countries, it has been suggested that they exhibit all the internal problems of a socialist state. From an economic standpoint the optimum size of a business unit may vary, depending on conditions in a particular industry.

Also on the unfavorable side, size confers disproportionate power and therefore limits the freedom of others. Since the centers of power control supply, they can influence price to the point of greatest profitability. This is a form of public exploitation. Even in a period of declining sales, suppliers can now raise prices instead of cut them. Because of administered prices we can now have inflation and recession at the same time, a combination that was theoretically impossible in a free market. By production policy and public relations activities, near-monopolies can create consumer demand, thus reversing the proper flow of influence between corporation and consumer. In view of the purpose of industry, the legitimacy of the authority of management disappears if it is not responding to genuine consumer interests.

Corporate concentration brings both efficiency and exploitation. As Galbraith has put it, "The foreign visitor, brought to the United States to study American production methods and associated marvels, visits the same firms as do attorneys of the Department of Justice in their search for monopoly." [10] Because of this amalgam between the desirable and the undesirable we have never been quite sure what to do about the problem of economic concentration. We cannot hesitate much longer.

Bigness spawns bigness. Big business has seen a parallel development in big labor as an attempt at a kind of countervailing power. Alongside these various forms of centralization, government has taken a more powerful initiative in economic affairs. If one combines the services of federal, state, and local governments in the United States, they add up to approximately one quarter of all economic activity in the country. To be sure, a very large part of this is accounted for by national defense and space exploration, which are usually not considered particularly socialistic. Even so, government activity in our country can be calculated as greater than the government's share in such avowedly socialist countries as India, Sweden, or Norway.[11]

All the leading governments of the world have accepted major responsibility for maintaining full employment, along with economic stability and growth. The United States has also accepted sufficient regulation to make ours to a substantial degree a planned economy. We have fixed a framework of limits around private decisions. Profits and incomes are modified by taxation or minimum wage laws. Quality of some products is controlled through food and drug legislation. Business policies are modified by federal fiscal and monetary policy, as well as by regulatory legislation. The government also provides positive aids to economic activity in the form of loans, tariffs, or subsidies. It has accepted the obligation to provide an economic climate for prosperity for business enterprises and a minimal welfare for its citizens.

Along with all the social gains that have been made as a result of the interaction between government and business, there are also ominous threats mushrooming about us. One of these is the great concentration of power in the military-industrial complex. It has been estimated that the militarized portion of American capitalism accounts for 8 to 10 percent of the gross national product. Military expenditures during the 1960's have been larger than the total of all personal income taxes, have supplied one fourth of all federal public works, and have subsidized about one third of all research in the country.[12] Kenneth Boulding concludes, "The only place where creeping socialism has been significant in the United States is the Department of Defense." In terms of gross national product he finds the defense department the second-largest centrally planned economy in the world, after the Soviet Union and ahead of the People's Republic of China.[13]

Because of the numerous modifications introduced into classical capitalism, it has been variously suggested that our actual practice should be described as democratic capitalism, welfare capitalism, people's capitalism, or monopoly capitalism. More descriptively accurate, however, are those who prefer to call our present system a mixed economy, with a blending of a variety of private and governmental enterprises. We have pluralistic economic structures that defy the simple designations of the past. Yet at the same time that we have greatly modified our practices, our ideology to a great extent remains the same. We suffer from "image lag" as we desperately pretend to live in a world that no longer exists. To update our ideology, and even more important, to resolve bitter debates about how we should modify our pluralistic mix, requires depth understanding of the three basic issues of ownership, motivation, and control. These are the foundational elements that determine the shape of any economic structure.

THE PRIVATIZATION OF PROPERTY

When we speak of the ownership of property, we are talking about a socially defined right of exclusive control and disposition. I decide what to do with whatever I own. In any culture, such a property right is a grant from society, either through the informal definitions of custom or the formal decisions of the political community. On this basis a great variety of forms of ownership have been historically accepted. Among the earliest cultures known to us, hunting grounds or even canoes might be equally accessible to every member of the tribe. In our own time we consider it appropriate that some forms of property, like highways, should be socially owned, while we protect the private ownership of houses or consumer goods. Classical capitalist economic theory makes much of the private ownership of almost all producer goods, like factories and machines. Private ownership in such cases may be held either by single individuals or by limited groups, as in partnerships or corporations. No such system of property rights is necessarily inherent in the nature of reality. As Blackstone pointed out in his *Commentaries on the Laws of England,* "There is no foundation in nature or in natural law, why a set of words upon parchment should convey the dominion of land; . . . or why the occupier of a particular field or of a jewel, when lying on his death-bed, and no longer able to maintain possession, should be entitled to tell the rest of the world which of them should enjoy it after him." [14] Grants of property rights are made to suit the purposes of society because they are expected to produce the ends that particular society considers desirable. As Tawney pointed out, ownership ought never to be absolute, but always conditional, tested by the function it performs.[15] A survey of major theories concerning the basis for property rights will make the meaning of this clear and provide the basis for our own current judgments.

One group of theories is based on social utility. The utilitarians typically based property rights on their tendency to promote the public good. The church fathers emphasized property as the creation of God for the common use of all men and made this the basis for the ultimate desirability of common ownership. Characteristically, they then accepted the present necessity for private property to safeguard against the social consequences of man's tendency toward evil. Augustine saw greed as leading to unacceptable disorder unless private property rights were defined. Aquinas added the necessity in human law of private property to provide incentive. Both Augustine and Aquinas insisted that the right to property depended upon using it rightly. Aquinas elaborated the proposition that property, though owned privately, should be used as though it were held in common. Aquinas insisted that possessions that were superfluous belonged to those who needed them. For this reason, if the rich did not share with the poor, he argued that the poor might even steal such superfluities to meet their own needs.[16] Private rights could not override the common right of mankind for the necessities of life.

A second group of theories sees property as essential to the development of personality. Aristotle, for example, defended private property as an effective stimulus to character and personal effort. He held that under communism one could not exercise the two important virtues of self-control and liberality. Hegel saw property as an extension of personality, saying, "To appropriate is at bottom only to manifest the majesty of my will toward things." Brunner saw property as necessary to freedom. He wrote: "The man who has nothing at his disposal cannot act freely. . . . The man who treads on strange ground, touches strange property at every movement he makes is not a free man." [17]

Brunner saw, however, that the property which confers freedom on some may destroy the freedom of others. If a man denies this right to others because he claims too much for himself, he robs God and neighbor. Whatever personality values property confers are the right of every man. For this reason Hobhouse observed, "Ethical individualism in property, carried through, blows up its own citadel." In the case of some kinds of property it may be that individual fulfillment is best served by shared ownership, as in the case of a large state park in addition to a private yard, or a public library in addition to a personal bookshelf.

Another approach is the fruit-of-labor theory. As developed by John Locke, this holds that whatever a man "removes out of the state that Nature hath provided and left it in, he hath mixed his labour with it, and joined to it something that is his own, and thereby makes it his property." The work of gathering apples makes them the property of the gatherer. There are limitations, however, to the amount a person has a right to appropriate. One limitation is that there should be "enough, and as good left in common for others." Another is that "as much as any one can make use of to any advantage of life before it spoils, so much he may by his labour fix a property in." If a man takes so many apples that they rot, he is a thief.[18]

Hobhouse has pointed out that, while private property may under certain conditions secure for a worker the fruits of his toil, under other conditions it may become a means of excluding the mass of the people from the means for earning a livelihood.[19] There is the further difficulty of determining whose labor is responsible for modern products. Entire groups mix their labor with commodities. The car at the end of the assembly line belongs to everyone in the factory; and what about the suppliers of electricity to the plant, or the police who protected the property, or the taxpayers who paid the police? Since we no longer live in the simple handicraft days of scythes and cobbler's benches, ultimately, in one way or another, the whole community takes part in production, and this could be used as an argument for socialism. Indeed, Karl Marx drew just this conclusion on the basis of his labor theory of value.

A fourth and last approach might be labeled the divine purpose theory. Or, secularists may prefer to speak of ultimate meaning or transcendent purpose. Whatever the form of words, this emphasizes that the goods of this world have significance as part of a larger whole than man, nature, and their relationships. Property is the gift of God. Ownership is a derived, not an inherent right. We are to use property for the purposes of God in the well-being of all men.

A sovereign God is the creator and owner of all property. "The earth is the LORD's." (Ps. 24:1.) "All things come from thee, and of thy own have we given thee." (I Chron. 29:14.)

Some Biblical writings pushed this even to the extreme year-of-jubilee proposal that land should not be sold in perpetuity (Lev. 25:23). Throughout church history the doctrines of creation and sovereignty have led to the consistent assertion that man can claim no absolute ownership. Human rights are derivative and conditional, a delegation of God's original claim. God gives man the free use of material goods (Gen. 1:26–29), but ultimate ownership remains in His hands. The Biblical injunction is to beware of the pride of possession (Deut. 8:11–18). When a man uses property primarily for private purposes he is a fool (Luke 12:16–21).

Since man is not the absolute owner, he is to administer God's resources as a trustee for the beneficiaries of the trust, namely all mankind. Christian ethical insight has emphasized the obligation incurred by ownership. There is less of a right to enjoy than there is a duty to serve. The purposes of God to be realized through human management include the fullest possible actualization of the highest potentialities of man. That system of property is best which contributes most to those ends. Like the observance of the sabbath (Mark 2:27), all our legal definitions of ownership must become functional. Man is not made for property, but property is made for man. This approach would use tests such as those suggested by the social utility and extension-of-personality theories of property, but it would place such tests in the larger setting of transcendent meanings for life under God. The highest usages of property are as a means for developing ethical and spiritual values. Jesus, in his enjoyment of material creation, stood against absolute asceticism, but he also opposed radical secularism. He clearly saw that man was not to live by bread alone and that his life did not consist in his possessions (Matt. 4:4, Luke 12:15). He was to seek first of all the kingdom of God and, if necessary for that purpose, to sell all his possessions (Matt. 6:33, 13:44–46). The same robust radicalism applies to devoting all the property we have to human fulfillment. Calvin insisted that a man defrauds his neighbors unless he remembers that "the only limit of his beneficence is the failure of his means." [20] Much of what we are accustomed to hear defended as legitimate rights of property the Bible would call robbery of God and grinding the faces of the poor.[21]

A second aspect of the purpose of God is that the benefits of property should be available to all. This adds to the functional test a democratic principle. Every man is to be given opportunity for access to such property as he needs. This basic human right includes more than possible use of property owned by someone else. Whatever values are associated with private ownership as such, these are to be shared by all men. Pope John XXIII, in his encyclical *Mater et magistra*, continued the emphasis of previous great encyclicals when he said, "It is not enough, then, to assert that man has from nature the right of privately possessing goods as his own, including those of productive character, unless, at the same time, a continuing effort is made to spread the use of this right through all ranks of the citizenry." He also recognized that private property might not meet this test, as when producer goods "carry with them power too great to be left in private hands, without injury to the community at large." [22]

Fletcher called this requirement of equal opportunity "the principle of universal human equities." In view of God's creation, "all men have an inalienable share in the patrimony." [23] In more theological language, this is summarized in a prayer of Anselm: "O Eternal God, one Father of all, who teachest us by reason that all the riches of the world are made by Thee for man's common use, and that by natural law not one of them belongs to one man more than to another; direct us, we pray Thee, in obedience to Thy law, that all things may serve all men, to the increase of Thy glory." [24]

Criteria such as these just outlined will not allow us to become absolutist about either private or social ownership. Not only are there different forms of property but their consequences may differ under varying circumstances. Four general forms of ownership can be distinguished: (1) private ownership and control, as in the food on our kitchen shelves; (2) private ownership and social control, as the speed of cars or the regulated rates of gas companies; (3) social ownership and control, as in the military establishment or various public corporations; (4) social ownership and private control, as in state industry under totalitarianism managed by a small elite, or war plants in a democracy owned by government but managed by private industry. Types of property might be classified into consumer goods, distribution agencies, means of production, raw materials, and media of communication. If we accept the ultimate purpose of property relationships to be the physical, social, and spiritual fulfillment of all men, ethical exploration must ask regarding any given type of property what form of ownership under a given set of circumstances best meets the functional and the democratic tests. We can here illustrate the issues involved in a few general and preliminary statements. These may point promising directions for the future, even though they need to be reviewed in any particular instance.

There are strong reasons for the almost universal privatization of consumer goods. This is almost a matter of definition. If ownership is to be defined as control over ultimate disposition, then consumer goods that are ready to be used up would of necessity be in private hands. Furthermore, freedom in the use of consumer goods is especially important for providing the essential material base for higher personality development. Even here, however, a minimum of social regulation becomes necessary in order to prevent the use of goods in such a way that would have an adverse effect upon the welfare or the liberty of other persons.

The means of distribution, or wholesale and retail outlets, are the face of the economic process that is closest to consumers. The operation of retail organizations can be most closely observed in their neighborhood units. The argument for an extension of consumer cooperatives becomes particularly strong at this point, provided that practical considerations for maintaining them can be met.

The media of mass communication are deeply involved with the public interest. Their accuracy, cultural quality, and freedom for expression are essential considerations in a democracy. It would appear to many that these characteristics are best protected by private ownership, although this argument grows weaker as control of the media becomes concentrated, and as the media become disproportionately accessible to narrow economic interests and political factions. If either the enforcement of professional codes by the industries themselves or strict public regulation breaks down, this strengthens the argument for social ownership of some media—either of entire industries or of pilot projects to be used as "yardsticks."

The manufacturing sector of the economy takes in a lot of territory. A variety of treatments might be appropriate in different segments. When monopolies or near-monopolies exploit those for whom they produce, the public must deal with them in one of the ways listed in Chapter 4. The public interest is also dominant in those forms of production which are basic, i.e., extremely vital to the total economy. For example, unless the railroad, steel, and power industries are in good shape, the entire economy drastically suffers. Here again the arguments for some form of stronger social control become more convincing. Then there are certain productive enterprises that require more capital than private industry is willing to invest or that do not allow the possibility of the usual kind of profit return. In such matters as flood-control dams or low-cost housing the public initiative becomes more important. Apart from these distinctive types, the remainder of manufacturing industries may well continue to be privately owned. The value of diversity, freedom to deviate, or the desirability of a large private enterprise sector may well be the decisive consideration, leaving a major sector of manufacturing in private hands with such minimal social regulation as is necessary.

Among the unique characteristics of raw materials and natural resources is the fact that they are the gift of nature, comparatively unmixed with human labor. Furthermore, their conservation is essential to the welfare of future generations. The chief among them are certainly basic to the total economy, and the arguments used for basic industries would also seem to apply here. Land is a unique natural resource in that it can become not only a factor in production but also in a real sense a consumer good. Walking in the yard or growing flowers around one's home is a value that necessitates private control. Another complication, pointed out by Henry George and others, is that the technical rental value of land as such involves unearned increment. (The technical definition of rent excludes payments for such functions as managerial service or capital investment.) The value of a location as such is largely due to the action of other persons who make it more desirable. When others move into an area the value of a piece of land goes up. It seems particularly unjust that succeeding generations should reap the benefits of some ancestor's possession of a lot in the middle of Manhattan island rather than on the great plains of Nebraska. There is a strong argument for a tax totally recovering for society such unearned increment. Or, why should a landowner reap wealth from an oil strike unrelated to his own effort and so unexpected that it had not entered into his purchase price for the property? At least, if he claims such a bonanza, he can no longer object to handsome payments to the idle poor. A more objective observer might prefer to withhold munificent rewards from both those who refuse to work and those who have not worked.

The expansion of this kind of analysis would lead to a mixed pattern of ownership. Ours is for the most part a private property system. We also have a vast amount of social ownership that we take for granted, including schools, libraries, parks, fire and police departments, highways, sewage systems, the military complex, the Panama Canal, and many others. Some forms of social ownership may have become anachronistic and should be transferred into private hands. On the other hand, some of our major problems may be best met by a shift toward social ownership. On this whole matter we have been greatly handicapped by our preference for an absolutist or doctrinaire approach rather than pragmatic and specialized decision.

ALTRUISTIC ETHICS AND ACQUISITIVE MOTIVES

What are the incentives that can sufficiently impel men to economic participation? The reliance of capitalism in both its classical and modified forms is on the acquisitive motive. This is broader than the so-called "profit motive," because it applies to all participants in the economic process. Not only owners but also workers, consumers, and professional persons are expected to act in such a way as to maximize their own satisfactions. Reliance on automatic adjustments through a market price assumes that they will do so.

On the face of it, this contradicts the major religious and ethical systems of the world, which stress altruistic outgoing concern. As one's most important or controlling motivation, service to others is given priority over satisfying oneself. For the loving person, the most important purpose of enhancing the self is that it enables him better to serve others. Love is given a radical meaning as directed to all persons without exception and as accepting unlimited liability even to the point of self-sacrifice. The advocates of the acquisitive motive may assume that by serving self, one's action also serves others. Jesus stressed the opposite. He made it clear that it is only by placing others first that, as an unsought by-product, is it possible to gain one's own highest fulfillment (Matt. 16:25). The meaning of an economic vocation is then found primarily in its contribution to others. The acquisitive approach to the selection of an occupation searches for the greatest personal reward for which individual abilities can somehow be made to qualify. The altruistic approach looks for the greatest social need to which one's personal capacities can contribute.

Many of the defects of our current culture, which foreshadow a calamitous future, grow out of the prominence given to the acquisitive motive. Dishonesty and manipulation, as in deceptive advertising or shoddy goods, become powerful temptations to the profit-seeker. One might paraphrase Lord Acton and suggest that the pursuit of money corrupts, and the bigger the money, the more absolute the corruption. Egoism is inherently exploitative, for the interests of others are given only secondary consideration. When one chooses the easiest job with sufficiently high pay, instead of working up to his highest capacity at the point of greatest social need, he is robbing society. Most of us would not want to be treated by a doctor who considered it a chore to do the job and was happy only when he received his check or bought a new boat. We would refuse to vote for a presidential candidate who was in it only for the money. G. K. Chesterton was basically right when he suggested that in searching for lodgings it is more important to know the landlady's philosophy of life than it is to see the room.

Acquisitive motives also become personally destructive. Psychiatrists have long noted that one root of serious emotional disturbance is the glaring contradiction between accepted ethical teachings and the requirement of an acquisitive economy. More than that, for so-called normal persons self-interest is a form of introversion. It tends to narrowness of outlook, psychological deterioration, or even the destruction of the self. When anyone in the modern world insists that he needs luxury, one can be certain that such a person will neither be deeply happy nor fulfilled (compare Mark 8:36). Yet an acquisitive system conditions men to be self-seeking. Selfishness becomes self-perpetuating. Custom stimulates egoistic drives latent in us all. In a society in which the security of an individual and his family depends on egoistic behavior, widespread patterns of aggression and aggrandizement are inevitable. Such a society, so long as it simultaneously maintains higher ethical generalizations, is at war with itself.

Contradictory consequences appear within the economic system itself. Acquisitive drives disturb the stability of the free market that they are intended to protect. For example, the avoidance of depression or business losses requires that production or expansion or savings not go beyond the optimum point that is supported by current demand. It is to any individual enterpriser's self-interest that, on the one hand, total production not pass beyond that optimum point, but that, on the other hand, his own share of that production be as large as possible. In individually pursuing the second end, it is inevitable that producers together should periodically violate the first end. This has been illustrated in the parable of the nine ships and the one cargo. A cargo went to each of nine shipowners in turn asking to be carried. It being a time of business prosperity, no one of them had an available ship. After the cargo departed, each shipowner reasoned that if he built another ship he could increase his business and make additional profit. The result was that nine ships were built but only one cargo was available to be carried.

The inherent inefficiencies of an acquisitive system were overlooked by Adam Smith when he argued, "It is not from the benevolence of the butcher, the brewer, or the baker, that we expect our dinner, but from their regard to their own interest." In one of the most widely quoted passages in *The Wealth of Nations*, Smith said: "He intends only his own gain, and he is in this, as in many other cases, led by an invisible hand to promote an end which was no part of his intention. . . . By pursuing his own interest he frequently promotes that of the society more effectually than when he really intends to promote it." [25] Economists have aptly observed that this "invisible hand" has become increasingly invisible. From the standpoint of ethical theory it has always been nonexistent, except for the most narrow range of circumstances. As Tawney put it, the idea that the expression of individual interest produced the social welfare is a "compound of economic optimism and moral bankruptcy." [26] Under frontier conditions, when the wilderness is large and the population small, each man may clear as much acreage as he wishes and society's desire for farmland may still be served. This was what Kenneth Boulding called the "cowboy economy." But under modern corporate conditions the advantages of egoistic striving often are more quickly outweighed by the disadvantages. We are now in a "spaceman economy," crowded into spaceship earth, with limited resources and subject to a more immediate social impact by private acts.[27]

There is one major and decisive argument in favor of a limited appeal to acquisitive motives. Men as they exist are not yet able to respond with the kind of radical love described above. The cynic remarks that under capitalism man exploits man, while under communism it is the other way around! Even with a more optimistic view, or with the hope that more-liberated persons may emerge as part of a super-industrial civilization, men would still not be free of the ambivalent potentialities that characterize basic human nature. It is hard to get dishes washed even in an idealistic commune. Institutional structures cannot move farther ahead than the personnel that is to man them. If we were to begin to rely completely on non-acquisitive motives, the wheels of industry would grind to a halt before tomorrow morning. There is always a cost to selfishness, but it may be necessary to pay part of this price in order effectively to motivate enough persons to economic participation.

Yet the ethical and economic prescription is clear. Comparatively speaking, we need to move in the direction of a greater reliance on more altruistic motives. It is increasingly essential to move as far in the direction of dependence on altruism as is possible, given the human situation of which all of us are a part. The question is how far we can go in that direction and still retain sufficient incentive. For an answer to this question we need to turn to psychological research as well as to history and economic experience.

No serious student of the subject would deny the great complexity of human motivation. A wide variety of needs and interests may become roots of action. These needs and interests (or desires) could be listed on a chart. The list would include the desire for material gain and also the desire for power, emotional ecstasy, the good conscience, or a variety of experience. Alongside each of these might appear manifestations or varieties of these desires, running in a continuum from the more grossly egoistic, through expressions of mutuality (or equal regard for self and others), to the more completely altruistic. To illustrate this continuum with respect to only two of the desires on our list, let us consider the desire for material gain and the desire for status or power.

With respect to the desire for material gain, the most dangerously antisocial drive is the desire for personal and family wealth, regardless of the consequences for other persons. Also egoistic, but less devastating, is the desire for security. Moving along the chart to the category of mutuality of concern, we note that many men are motivated by an interest in creative work. They egoistically enjoy activity, but their satisfaction is also enhanced because they see their activity as significant in making a social contribution. Many managers illustrate this motivation when they speak of the inner satisfaction of having done a good job or the thrill of coordinating an enterprise. The same motivation has loomed large among scientists in a laboratory or doctors in the operating room. This becomes the more altruistic as one is moved by a recognition of the importance of his product. His motivation is then production for use not only by himself but also by others. This concern in its most altruistic form becomes the service motive, or the dominant desire to meet human need. This has characterized many somewhat saintly persons who often in obscure circumstances have subordinated their own interests to meeting family crises or aiding a needy humanity.

Our suggested chart also lists the desire for status or power. The most socially dangerous egoistic drive here becomes the desire to dominate others, as in the case of a political dictator or an old-fashioned business tycoon. Less devastating, though still egoistic, is the desire for autonomy or independence as an individual. Or one may work because this is the socially accepted thing to do. Society looks down on the drone, and one wants to be well thought of. Moving into the category of mutuality are the desires related to social participation. One is affected by the morale of the group and in turn helps to sustain the efforts of others. This involves a shared status and a kind of informal democratic decision. Much of the effort expended by a work group is in conformity with this kind of group expectation. This may become identification with the goals of the group. One works harder as he shares the common purpose of those in the mission control center of getting a space capsule back safely, or of a population in keeping democracy strong against totalitarianism. At its altruistic end this continuum includes a desire to contribute to the status of others. While this is a comparatively rare commodity as a dominant motive, it does enter into the incentive of many a secretary of an executive, staff member of a church, leader of a growth group, or subordinate political appointee.

To be true to the multiple motivation of man, other desires might be added to the chart proposed above. The ones discussed are enough, however, to suggest that popular beliefs and practices lag behind the possibilities. We have exaggerated the extent to which the more egoistic appeals are necessary, and we have overlooked the extent to which nonacquisitive motives actually exist. Business administrators now realize that reliance on financial incentives releases but a fraction of the cooperation of workers. The motivation of most workers is in the range of a desire for security or social acceptance, or interest in creative work or social participation. Studies in industrial psychology have shown nonacquisitive incentives to be more important than we have often thought.

The relationship between the profit motive and management incentive is also becoming more obscure. Profits in the technical sense are distributed to shareholders or plowed back as internally produced capital into the enterprise. Management does not directly participate in profits. While there is considerable emphasis on handsome compensation for management, even here there is no close relationship between salary and effort expended. The president of a struggling small company may use more energy and skill to keep it going than the much more highly paid executive of a large corporation. Other large groups are also less moved by clearly egoistic motives—including scientists, administrators of public enterprise or welfare agencies, and teachers or many other professional people. Groups such as these are becoming more important as we increasingly turn from goods to services, and as the knowledge and skills of the technician and the coordinator become more vital to economic life.

Furthermore, in days of comparative affluence when basic needs are largely met, acquisition no longer remains so compelling an incentive. A satisfied need is not a motivation for behavior. While persons generally are not wholly disinterested in the level of their income, in an economy of plenty other personal desires and the goals of the group can become more prominent as motives. In times of comparative material abundance, needs or interests on a higher ethical level may begin to dominate behavior. We have not begun to give adequate thought to the implications of this.[28]

We do now as a matter of realistic fact find that it is possible to rely on a broad mixture of motives. We resort to compulsion in drafting members of military forces at low pay. We operate VISTA and the Peace Corps with Schweitzer and Thoreau types, nonconformists who do not move to the beat of the high-wage drums. If ours is a mixed economy, it has also been characterized by a mixture of motives. Ethical and economic experience both suggest that our motivational problem still remains one of moving from the prevailing reliance on egoistic incentives to a greater reliance on altruistic incentives as fast as the human material manning the economic institution can stand the strain. This might mean three things more specifically. We need to continue to regulate by law (or by professional codes of ethics, advisory commissions of consumers, or ethical watchdogs on boards of directors) the most socially dangerous manifestations of the most grossly egoistic drives. This would include such things as pure food and drug laws, securities and exchange regulation, advertising codes, more progressive income taxation, or antimonopoly action. In the second place, we could encourage alternative forms that place greater reliance on less egoistic motives. These might include consumer cooperatives, public-spirited labor unions and management associations, or an extension of civil service practices. Never to be neglected is a third and very basic requirement for a more promising future. Social programs at this point must be supplemented by more effective programs for personal change. Churches and schools cannot escape the responsibility for producing more altruistic persons who are prepared to work creatively because of sensitivity to need and dedication to service.

CONTROVERSY ABOUT COMPETITION

The process of regulation in a capitalist society and in a large part of our present economy is competition. A businessman may freely adopt such policies as he wants, and a worker may apply for any job without restraint, so long as each can meet the competition. A gasoline station owner can get by with simply pumping gasoline until the station on the next corner reduces prices or begins cleaning windshields. Freedom of vocational choice is protected for everyone, provided that a better qualified person does not get there first. This kind of control among otherwise freely acting independent units is in contrast with a participatory procedure for making joint decisions through some form of system-wide planning.

Numerous benefits have been claimed for this aspect of "free enterprise." It supposedly supplements the acquisitive motive as an incentive to improve efficiency. To stay ahead of competitors one must work energetically, eliminate waste, and adopt the best available methods. Competitive processes help to select the competent, leading to the survival of the fittest. At the same time, competition theoretically controls the profit motive, preventing runaway exploitation. If prices become unduly high, someone will try to attract more business by cutting his price. Competition is an essential part of the market mechanism for coordinating many complex economic relationships. Hayek insists that it is "the only method by which our activities can be adjusted to each other without coercive or arbitrary intervention of authority." [29]

The full consequences of competitive controls include items not covered by this optimistic theory. Competition is a win-lose mechanism. The unsuccessful suffer, and sometimes through no fault of their own. Chance or accident plays a part in survival. Those eliminated are not necessarily unfit for superior production. They may simply be unfit for the types of deceit or manipulation necessary for success in some competitive areas. As well as stimulating improvement, competition can pull all to the level of the lowest. So long as consumers do not have research funds or testing laboratories, misleading advertising or shoddy merchandising may have to be imitated for even an honest man to stay in business. Baumhart[30] shows how moderate competition increases ethical conduct in business, while too much decreases ethical conduct. Furthermore, competition presupposes many small units. Technologically these may be quite inefficient. Duplication often leads to waste and to serious loss for consumers.

Even worse for the theory, the most efficient competitors do not remain small. Success in competition tends to eliminate competition. The consequences include inequality, insecurity, and undemocratic concentrations of control. Too widespread reliance on competition weakens the possibility for consciously adopting common goals by an entire public. Recent emphases in group dynamics and the human potential movement have demonstrated superior possibilities for stimulus and control in collaborative instead of conflict styles. Anthropologists and social psychologists have noted greater group cohesion where societies work together for the common good.

That there should be such ambivalent consequences for economic competition comes as no surprise to the ethicist. Particularly when this form of control is combined with the acquisitive motive, there would seem to be a prima-facie case against competition, to the effect that competition is contradictory to love expressed as cooperation or fraternity. As a general guideline or goal, it is better that men should work together cooperatively for common goals than that they should compete for diverse goals. "Every man for himself and the devil take the hindmost" reflects the law of the jungle and conflicts with the rule, "You shall love your neighbor as yourself" (Matt. 22:39). The spirit expressed in "Love your enemies" (Matt. 5:44) would seem to lead to action for enhancing the opponent instead of injuring him. It is reprehensible to get ahead at the expense of another. Win–lose games, wherever possible, are to be replaced by win–win procedures. Always unfinished on society's agenda is the business of finding more satisfactory structural forms for brotherhood. We have developed some organizational patterns for cooperation, as in the family, or business corporations, or political units. In the overall economy or in international relations we have some distance to go with respect to devising a framework for supporting rather than obstructing each other.

To be sure, there is within the Judeo-Christian faith an intense individualism. Finally it is the person in his aloneness who stands before God. It is individuals who receive the gracious gifts of God. Every man is to act autonomously in his decision-making. His is always a responsible individualism, however. He is to make his decisions with a sense of obligation for the entire community. Private ends are to be subordinated to the common good. There is also within our religious heritage an intense collectivism. Great importance is attached to the group, whether it be Israel, the disciples, or the early church. The unity described in the twelfth chapter of Romans and of I Corinthians, which made those within the early church "members one of another," also came to be considered as a prototype for an ideal society in which all would share such intimacy.

The synthesis between individualism and collectivism was to be made through responsible individuals living the life of radical love. Again this presupposes a quality of existence that is not yet sufficiently present in a realistic world. Again we would not expect to eliminate competition, but we would work at keeping it within bounds and at discovering specific areas within which broader cooperation might be an immediate possibility. What this might mean more specifically for our time will be discussed in a later chapter.

While there are areas in which total autonomy is desirable, it is not always true that the community is better off if individuals are left completely free to compete with each other. On major policy decisions shaping the destinies of all, individuals are best served as through the democratic community they set shared goals. The specialists in the technostructure need to be interfered with at the point of goals. Just as war is too important to be left to the generals and political policies are too important to be left to the politicians, so the basic elements in choice between alternative futures are too important to be left to the economically powerful.

FREEING UP FREEDOM

The issue of unrestricted individual freedom versus consciously adopted social controls also has political ramifications that are reciprocally related to economic practices. For political structures also there are profound roots for an ethical insistence upon freedom. If one holds any of a variety of forms of theism, he can say that human freedom is a grant from God. Man is not jerked about by the deity as a puppet is manipulated, responding only to tugs on its strings. God desires a relationship of fellowship that is possible only with a free being, not with a puppet. God has given man freedom to respond or to rebel. When a political dictator attempts totalitarian control of the most basic aspects of a man's life, he sets himself up to do what God himself chooses not to do.

The case for liberty is also rooted in the nature of man. Human beings can fulfill the purpose of their beings only by making responsible choices. There is essential worth and un-realized potentiality in each person. The full realization of this possibility requires considerable autonomy. Society exists to a great extent to give persons opportunity to actualize their destinies. Every man also has vast potentialities for evil. Another function of society is to protect all from the perversities of each. This means freedom from control by both the criminal and the arbitrary ruler. No person or group should be given unchecked power over others. Dictators are diabolical partly because they do not allow the balancing of power among imperfect men that is necessary to approximate justice. Reinhold Niebuhr's epigram deserves its frequent repetition: "Man's capacity for justice makes democracy possible; but man's inclination to injustice makes democracy necessary." [31]

Important as freedom is, it can never be absolute. The liberties of one are always conditioned by the equal claims of others. In economic affairs, for example, freedom of occupational choice and of consumers' choice are always in tension with each other. Large numbers of applicants can become professional opera singers only if enough consumers are willing to attend operas. In political affairs I should not be left free to deny the freedoms of others. The social goal then becomes not absolutizing liberty, but rather maximizing it to the fullest degree possible.

The path of the centuries has been worn smooth by three different vehicles for the maximization of freedom. The first of these vehicles, or approaches to the maximization of freedom, is benevolent autocracy, or the rule of the well-intentioned few. Continued tribute has been paid to this model by a wide variety of elitist practitioners. Organizational theory, like politics, makes strange bedfellows—including in this particular bed communism, fascism, Roman Catholic or other hierarchical religious bodies, and capitalist paternalism. Both communism and fascism have claimed that they were representing the genuine aspirations of the people and were providing conditions that broadened the range of popular choice. Popes and paternalists have also insisted that others were more free to do what they really wanted if someone who knew better than they made the decisions as to what they actually needed. In spite of such reassuring words, rule by the few is a contradiction of freedom for the many. Furthermore, there is no way to ensure that the most efficient and benevolent person will get into the position of leadership, and there is no consistently orderly and effective way of handling the problem of succession to the throne. Dolts have often followed geniuses. Even the best of autocrats is still a seriously imperfect ruler, because he does not allow liberty. Whatever values may be realized under autocracy, freedom is not one of them. As a path to liberty this is a dead-end street.

A second appealing approach taken to maximize freedom is that of anarchy. On the surface of things it would appear that there could be no greater maximization of liberty than to allow each person to do what was right in his own eyes without external restraint. This would indeed allow full liberty if all men were completely well informed, wise, and altruistic. The perfect political system might be described as the anarchy of love. It has been suggested that there are no laws in heaven. The obvious rejoinder is that those who go there are selected rather carefully! This somewhat frivolous suggestion nevertheless points to the Achilles heel of anarchism, whether advocated by older philosophers such as Kropotkin and Tolstoi, or by a segment of modern youth culture. Given men as they are and as they will continue to be for some distance beyond the foreseeable future, anarchy cannot be self-sustaining.[32]

This is illustrated in the frontier community before the advent of established law. Every man could then do what he considered to be desirable, but it was not long before the most unscrupulous or the most fortunate or the most efficient in handling his gun fastened his rule on others. Most citizens could then exercise their freedom only at the sufferance of the dominant few. The same sequence is illustrated in laissez-faire capitalism and in national sovereignty. To a significant degree both of these are expressions of anarchy. When economic enterprisers were left free to act in their own interests, various combinations of efficiency and moral indifference led to the growth of large-scale business combines, which effectively terminated the freedom of small businessmen. Likewise, lack of international structures to restrain expressions of narrow national interest led to control by superpowers, with lesser nations losing control over their own destinies.

Anarchy, prematurely attempted, leads to its precise opposite —namely, autocracy. So long as men are not invariably brilliant as well as loving, it is necessary to protect the many against the excesses of the few. I have always been grateful for constitutional dicta that suggest that your freedom ends where my nose begins. My freedom has been much enhanced by such limitations on anarchy—and, of course, yours has too.

In a third path to freedom, the establishment of democracy, was found the solution for the dilemma of the frontier community. By democracy we mean a political structure characterized by (1) universal adult franchise on a one man–one vote basis; (2) the guarantee of civil liberties, allowing full participation in discussion; (3) majority decision, involving coercion of minorities by majorities instead of the opposite; and (4) protection of the rights of minorities to the fullest possible extent, not only by constitutional provision but by the self-restraint of majorities.[33] Maximum freedom is found in such a government of laws. Participation avoids the major defects of autocracy, and regulation eliminates the utopianism of anarchy. This has implications also for international relations and for economic life. In both cases we are slowly moving toward more democratic structures. To be sure, democracy presupposes a minimal basis of education and understanding, of character and common values, to allow reasonably sound public conclusions. Where these are not available, degrees of benevolent autocracy may be necessary. Yet, in our own society, democracy is the most promising structure for the maximization of liberty.

There is also a strong case to be made for democracy from the standpoint of an ethical concern for justice and order.

These too are functions of the state. It is important that each should be given his due within structures providing stability and dependability. Theoretically, justice and order can also be achieved under autocracy if the ruler is just and effective. We are now learning, however, that this is less likely, and that democracy is the system best calculated for maximizing not only liberty, but also justice and order. It is not true that dictatorships are more efficient. Recent insights into the group process underscore the advantages of democracy. The tyrant may be wrong, and there is no corrective when he is. He does not have the full, spontaneous participation of his people, since they do not feel "ownership" in established programs. The tyrant is also more likely to be wrong, since his decisions are not informed by widespread participation in free debate. The biases of those in power always need to be corrected by the views of those who lack power. Even the genius needs illumination from different perspectives. Autocracy prevents an inclusive group process from operating, stunts the moral and social development of citizens, and makes them less able to contribute in the future. In the short run, autocracy may be efficient under some circumstances, but in the long run, with a reasonably mature citizenry, democracy is likely to accomplish even more. In this general sense, for the system as a whole and in the long run, our choice is not freedom or order, but freedom *and* order.

IDENTIFYING TOTALITARIAN THREATS

Protection and enlargement of liberties require public understanding of basic threats that are now widely unrecognized. Rapid change and chronic crisis might now lead a confused and disillusioned population to accept an abrogation of liberties similar either to the communist combination of dictatorship with state-owned economic enterprise or the fascist form of totalitarianism plus a traditional economic system. While we have strong historical bulwarks against the rise of dictatorship, it is well to remember how quickly and unexpectedly such movements rose in other countries. Only a few months before he became head of the first Council of People's Commissars, Lenin was in exile in Switzerland, living in bare quarters in the home of a Zurich shoemaker. Only eight years before his triumph, Mussolini in almost a garret room founded his newspaper *Populo d'Italia*. After the elections of 1919, when not a single Fascist candidate was elected, Mussolini was described by his opponents as "a corpse to be buried in a ditch." Three years later he was dictator of Italy. In the elections of November, 1932, when the Nazi vote fell by over two million, opponents hailed this as "the final annihilation of Hitler." Three months later Hitler became chancellor.

Germany and Italy are particularly instructive as to how this can happen in industrialized nations with economic and political patterns generally similar to our own. In both countries there was widespread disappointment and suffering related to World War I. Continuing unemployment and economic hardship were intensified by the worldwide depression of the thirties. National crisis led to sharper conflict between numerous political factions. Growth in the parties of the left brought polarization also toward the right. Every German Reichstag under the Republic included representatives from ten to fifteen parties. The only way "splinter parties" could form a majority was by short-lived coalitions. Cabinet after cabinet failed as its support disintegrated. When no one could gain a parliamentary majority, German ministries were finally forced to govern by presidential decree. Intense conflict between opposing forces brought a wave of physical violence and terrorism. Black shirts or gray shirts and "red guards" paraded about and engaged in battles and beatings, riots and raids. The social picture was one of polarization and fragmentation, with insufficient support for any moderate program that might point a more constructive way out.

Crisis had its psychological aspects in threats to status, feelings of insecurity, nationalist loyalties, and frustrated ambitions. As Eugen Weber has put it, "Loss of hope in the possibilities of existing order and society, disgust with their corruption and ineffectiveness, above all the society's evident loss of confidence in itself, all these produce or spur a revolutionary mood in which the only issue lies in catastrophic action." [34] Disillusionment was joined with lack of any more ultimate faith that could point in decisive directions. The deepest crisis of all was a void in the souls of men, which led to a flight from freedom and a willingness to let dictators decide.

This kind of analysis sheds a great deal of light on the prospects for some form of totalitarianism in the United States. The question is not how many supporters of dictatorship are now influentially active in this country. There were not many members of fascist groups, for example, before the time of their rapid acceleration to power in Germany and Italy. The question to be faced is, rather, which groups in the United States would be expected quickly to support fascist-type measures in a time of serious national crisis. As Del Boca and Giovana have put it, "The American Radical Right must be judged not by its present composition . . . but by its function as a catalyser of all the active and latent reactionary forces in the country." [35] Herein lies one of our gravest social perils.

In dealing with this question, imagine the sort of breakdown that characterized pre-fascist Germany and Italy. This might come to us through one or more disasters, such as long continued economic depression, the beginning of the collapse of environmental support through pollution or resources depletion, the failure of society or even of the liberals within it to move from a boring and meaningless materialistic affluence to a new quality of life, a series of defeats for American foreign policy, or warfare that is long extended, decimating, or that results in national defeat. Some believe that such a crisis is already upon us. They point to the threat of nuclear war and environmental collapse, loss of confidence in basic institutions, a deep frustration about Vietnam, and a strong polarization over racial issues. Persistent problems and rapid change are threatening the status and hopes of large numbers of people. All these taken together may be creating a time ripe for a charismatic deliverer. The traditional "man on horseback" could now be replaced by a general in a jet, or a demagogue at the microphone.

Especially if crisis should become more serious, several large groups in our country, perhaps unintentionally, might assist in a dictator's takeover. An identification of such potential totalitarians must be responsibly made. There has been too much irresponsible accusation of persons as communists or fascists. No prediction is here made with respect to any specific individual. The point is that certain predispositions make it more likely that considerable numbers so characterized will give totalitarian groups the extra support or the passive assent necessary for their success.

Potential supporters of communist solutions might come from among those who tend to evaluate democratic freedom as less important than economic opportunity. If forced to a choice, some would prefer dictatorship with its illusion of rapid change over the slower processes of democracy—or they might be completely disillusioned with the possibility of any democratic change toward freedom and opportunity. Another predisposing trait is the habit of disregarding the imperfections in communist nations, excusing them for the imperialism, prejudice, tyranny, or national interest that the same person shouts about very loudly when it is practiced by democratic countries. Such a person may feel friendly toward left-wing dictatorships that keep rightists in jail while he is utterly opposed to right-wing dictators who keep leftists in jail.

So far as potential fascism is concerned, one group that might lend support is composed of those who, when forced to make a choice, would prefer to change our political practices in the direction of dictatorship rather than to change our economic practices in the direction of greater social controls. They might continue to prefer to make neither change, but when present structures seem no longer viable they would be willing to endanger democracy as a necessary price for preserving essentially the economic *status* quo. Another group might be composed of those who in time of threatening widespread international breakdown would prefer to extend American power over other nations rather than to move in the direction of world government exerting limited joint power for the nations. Another major group of possible pre-fascists (or, in this case, also pre-communists) is composed of those who, when persuasion becomes difficult, quickly move toward pushing people around. Rather than being willing to invest extra imagination and energy in troublesome democratic processes, they are predisposed to dictating and dominating. Theirs is the kind of authoritarian personality that expresses a similarly aggressive life-style in various other relationships. They are the parents who slap at slight provocation, and the citizens who in foreign policy quickly land the marines.[36]

The threat of totalitarianism comes from a broader source than those who in severe crises might at least tacitly accept communist or fascist nostrums. There are extremists both on the right and the left, many of whom may never accept the presuppositions of totalitarianism, yet who are using tactics that undermine the defenses of the democracy they may even be trying to defend. Perhaps unwittingly, they help lay the roadway over which potential totalitarians may later move. This kind of extremism does not characterize all members of the old or the New Left, nor can it be attributed to responsibly analytical reactionaries. But in at least three characteristic manifestations, it is uncritically accepted by a larger section of the public than we can complacently disregard.[37]

The first identifying characteristic of such extremism is the use of false labeling that slanderously identifies the opponent with whatever is particularly unpopular at the moment. In the days of Joseph McCarthy this was communism. Today it may be violence and social disorder, perhaps linked to communism or fascism, thus producing a multiheaded demon. This tactic tends to become a creeping libel by label. It may be progressively extended to positions to which it applies even less.

For example, the radical rightist may attempt not only to link democratic socialism with communism but to link political liberalism with democratic socialism. Finally, he may try to pin the label of socialistic radicalism on much or all of the Democratic party. The leftist, on the other hand, stretches the label of repression or fascism progressively to cover rightist totalitarians, reactionaries, right-wing Republicans, and perhaps all Republicans. If an uncritical public is at all impressed by extremist designations, this leaves such a narrow range of options as to result in social stagnation and collapse. If we accept the extremists' suggestion that free expression should not be allowed to those labeled as dangerous, this also drastically narrows the area of tolerance within which full freedom of speech is allowed—and that is totalitarianism. Extremists pretend to protect progress and freedom, but to defend those values they use methods that demolish progress and freedom. The tactic of creeping libel is illustrated among leftist extremists by their blanket condemnation of the establishment as antihuman, exploitative, and oppressive. United States foreign policy is seen as utterly without redeeming social value. Both responsible conservatives and ardent liberals are regarded as among the enemy. Jerry Rubin wrote: "Nazism comes to Amerika [sic] as liberalism. . . . The right-wing menace exists—but it's not Wallace. It's the Kennedy liberals." [38] False labeling by rightists has often combined the old "soft on communism" with the new "soft on crime and violence" charge. Liberals have been pictured as supporting dissent that obstructs the police and rends communities with disorder. A 1970 election ad supporting Senator Murphy in California against John Tunney, accused Tunney in his vote against the District of Columbia Criminal Procedure Act of having voted against outlawing "Molotov cocktails" and against penalties for using bombs—even though Tunney's reasons for opposing the bill were quite different.

Also a libel by label is the charge that reputable church groups are somehow communistic. A notorious illustration is the opening sentence of a 1953 *American Mercury* article by J. B. Matthews: "The largest single group supporting the Communist apparatus in the United States today is composed of Protestant clergymen." [39] The heading of the first of two 1971 *Reader's Digest* articles charged that "the World Council of Churches is using church power and church funds to back insurrection in the United States and Africa." [40] Dr. Eugene L. Smith, executive secretary of the World Council's New York office, as part of a point-by-point reply, charged the *Digest* articles with "unsubstantiated charges, misstatements of fact, distorted reporting, quotation of statements out of context." He added, "The total effect is to present a false picture of the World Council of Churches." [41]

A second weapon in the extremist's attack is intimidation. Having insinuated their guilt, he also attempts to silence his opponents. Not by assassination or arrest but by imposing more subtle disabilities on others, he tries to gain a monopoly of expression for opinions like his own. Attaching a defaming label in itself makes the person labeled less likely to be listened to. He is more likely to find it uncomfortable or costly to continue his public participation. Additional pressure may be exerted when an individual is openly or implicitly threatened with loss of position or when a television station is threatened with loss of license. Again this is something other than the processes of a free society. The democratic way of dealing with opposition is to speak against it. The totalitarian way is to silence it.

Among leftists who flunk this test are those who shout down a speaker or break up the meeting. It is impossible to conduct dialogue by rhythmic chanting, or by forceful seizure of the microphone, or by presenting nonnegotiable demands, or by mistaking an epithet for an argument. Radical students who silence professors by threatening their cars on the parking lot or by disrupting classes are little different from reactionary donors on the Board of Trustees who try to discharge the dissenting professor. Extremists on the right have also used similar forms of intimidation and coercion to silence opposition. In

February, 1950, at Wheeling, West Virginia, Joseph McCarthy introduced the first act of "the nightmare decade" with the words, "I have here in my hand a list . . ." [42] The subsequent silencing of opponents and destruction of careers will long live in infamy. Yet a revival of the tragic drama is hinted in the recent suggestion that protesters should be separated from society as rotten apples are removed from the barrel.

Intimidation by investigation is another device for exerting a "chilling effect" on political participation by citizens who are all too reluctant at best and who want no trouble when they do become involved in civic affairs. Intimidation can be as simple as taking the license numbers of cars parked near particular meetings or as complicated as computerized dossiers. Particularly does it alter the traditional role of the military in American life when its agencies begin to accumulate files on civilian opponents to Pentagon policy. This begins to turn civilian control of the military into military control of civilians. Unless restricted, there are alarming possibilities in modern computer technology turned toward the invasion of privacy. Arthur R. Miller, a law professor doing specialized study of the problem, fears that the computer "may become the heart of a surveillance system that will turn society into a transparent world." [43] As he suggests, a dictatorship of data banks and dossiers rather than of hobnailed boots will be no less a dictatorship.

A third characteristic of extremist tactics also becomes the more serious as one views it in the light of the history of totalitarian movements. To forestall crisis, continuous improvement is essential, yet radicals to right and to left have been busy undermining basic institutions that are necessary for such a progressive and just society, such as schools, libraries, churches, or welfare agencies. Modern democratic action requires a high level of education and the capacity to evaluate rapid change in the light of reliable norms. The first is impossible without adequate schools and the second is unlikely without vital, prophetic churches. Yet both extreme left and right find it to their interests to weaken the university and the church. This can be done by reducing available support, or by planting sufficient doubts in the mind of the general public to create a vague distrust of these agencies.

Widely held in the extremist left is the conviction that existing institutions are so oppressive and corrupt that there is no hope for their rehabilitation. Withdrawing participation plus a direct and open attack are matters of revolutionary policy. Occasional extreme statements may incorporate the undisguised intention to hasten the collapse of these agencies. Jerry Rubin sounded the call: "Burn the flag. Burn churches. Burn, burn, burn. . . . The revolution has replaced the church as the country's moral authority." Speaking for those who are critical of abstract thinking and favorable toward emotion and action, he also wrote: "The goal of the revolution is to eliminate all intellectuals. . . . Our task is to destroy the university. . . . We are going to invade the schools and free our brothers who are prisoners. We will burn the buildings and the books." [44]

On the rightist fringe, the kind of position taken by the John Birch Society has led some persons to campaign to impeach liberal Supreme Court justices, to weaken public school curricula, or to curtail library purchases of forbidden books. With respect to religious groups, we quote from a speech given by Vice-President Agnew, April 28, 1970, at Fort Lauderdale, Florida, according to the official version distributed by his office. In speaking of "the children of affluent, permissive, upper-middle-class parents who learned their Dr. Spock and threw discipline out the window," he stated: "They are the children dropped off by their parents at Sunday school to hear the 'modern' gospel from a 'progressive' preacher more interested in fighting pollution than fighting evil—one of those pleasant clergymen who lifts his weekly sermons out of old newsletters from a National Council of Churches that has cast morality and theology aside as not 'relevant' and set as its goal on earth the recognition of Red China and the preservation of the Florida Alligator." When statements like this are made about responsible organizations whose critical and creative stimulus is essential to a free society, what are the consequences for a healthy democracy?

Franklin Littell, out of many years of scholarship in this area, including extensive experience with church movements in Germany, wrote: "There was a time in the history of the Weimar Republic when just a few hundred preachers and teachers could have saved the constitution and reduced the Communists (KPD) and fascists (NSDAP) to ineffectiveness. They waited tentatively, however, convinced that the best educated and most Christian people in the world (as they saw it) would never follow the demagogues who were polarizing the public opinion and destroying the middle ground of reasonable politics. They waited, objectively, until too late." [45]

4
DIRECTIONS FOR DECISION

AUGUST 15, 1971, may go down in history as the end of an American era. On that day President Richard Nixon announced to the nation the adoption of wage and price controls for dealing with the double threat of inflation and unemployment. On the surface this would appear to have been something of a Damascus Road experience, whether the light came from heaven or from somewhat more mundane sources. Such a major reversal of policy could only be an admission of past error and the adoption of what previously had been staunchly opposed. The historically remarkable thing about the event was that there was almost no opposition to the move. Is this August day to be etched as the date of death on the tombstone of free enterprise as an accepted ideology? As pointed out in Chapter 3, in a discussion of recent trends in our economy, our practice has not been laissez-faire for some time. Yet the air was filled with talk as though it were. Now with the widespread recognition that we must go beyond comparatively mild, conventional guidance to much more thoroughgoing controls over economic activity, it would seem to be almost impossible to gain much support for the ideological proposition that free enterprise is the primary reliance of our economy. Will any politicians in the future ever again dare to resurrect the old ideological description? Probably they will. Not all politicians are known for their contemporaneity. Will they be able to win a large following for this tired slogan? Probably not, except perhaps to an extremist movement in a time of severe crisis. Obviously, ours has become and in all likelihood will remain a mixed economy with a large private enterprise sector, but with major government controls.

It is still true that the various groups now accepting controls as a matter of obvious necessity are doing so with quite different ends in mind. Business wants to maintain a high level of aggregate demand to sustain profits, and it wants protection from disruptive revolution by malcontents. Labor wants government to cut profits and to plan for full employment. Scattered intellectuals and preachers want help toward reordered priorities and a new quality of life. Some have egalitarian while others have elitist goals. Is a higher priority to be given to enhancing the affluence of the fortunate or to removing the penury of the disprivileged? It makes a great deal of difference for whose ends planning is undertaken. It also makes a good deal of difference what the methods of planning are to be and how thoroughly they are to be employed. Even among those accepting the idea of government regulation, there is sharp disagreement about how much guidance is desirable. This will be the battleground for decision-making for a long time to come. How far down the road of a mixed economy do we propose to move? What is the proper role of government in economic life?

A Guide Through Current Controversy

Economic planning by democratic government can be defined as conscious coordination and control of important sectors of the economy by responsible public authorities. If governments are "to promote the general welfare," they must recognize responsibility for the economic well-being of citizens. The method for coherently relating resources to such goals is planning—whether we do it to get to the theater on time, to make a career more satisfying, or to eliminate war.

In mass society, where neighbors live considerably closer

than they did on the frontier farm, more plans must be made jointly. Robinson Crusoe cannot be duplicated on Manhattan island. At least on things like devising a unified highway or controlling the business cycle, we recognize the advantages of conscious, coordinated planning for a common end, as over against the independent pursuit of diverse and contradictory ends. No economist denies the necessity of some such centralized decision, even if only to enforce contracts or maintain the general rules of the economic game. No politically significant group advocates turning over the management of the army to unregulated private enterprise. The highly controversial issue is the question of how far government planning should extend, and what its purposes should be.

Most helpful here is a pro and con consideration of major arguments regarding government planning, under three headings. Under government planning, what tends to happen to individual initiative and responsibility, efficiency, and freedom?

One major test to apply to proposals for centralized planning is that of responsibility. Those who oppose extensions of government initiative argue that state action undermines individual initiative and responsibility. For those who might otherwise give voluntarily, it is argued that law coerces philanthropy. When funds to relieve poverty are accumulated through taxation, the autonomy of the giver is violated. Instead of thus weakening the roots of altruism, society ought to encourage the spontaneous action that nurtures moral growth. Furthermore, accumulation of resources though taxation punishes those who are most energetic and successful. Instead of allowing them to keep what their capabilities have gained, we decrease their motivation to use those capabilities fully. Society as a whole becomes the loser in this kind of game.

Opponents also see government action as demoralizing those who receive aid. Beneficiaries come to expect things to be done for them. Their symbol becomes the outstretched hand instead of the working arm. Thus it is argued that the unemployed will not look for work so long as their needs are being met by welfare. This destroys the conditions essential for character growth. Public policy undermines the pioneering spirit in American society, with its virtues of hard work, frugality, and thrift. Far from being outdated, it is argued, these qualities are even more essential amid the complex threats of modern civilization.

On the other hand, those who argue in support of state planning are likely to insist that proper government initiatives provide new channels for the expression of initiative and responsibility, in the only forms appropriate in a mass society. The dispensing of assistance is always morally hazardous both to those giving and to those receiving, whether it is initiated by a public or a private agency. Certain types of public welfare may be less of a demoralizing "handout" than private charity. In the case of social-security-type benefits, the recipient has paid in his share of the tax and is entitled to his benefits as much as the person who receives a check from an insurance company after a fire or auto accident. Paying a social security premium is a new form of expressing self-reliance. Furthermore, a major portion of the expenditure of tax-accumulated funds is made in planned support or subsidy of the enterprises of the privileged. They would scarcely admit to being demoralized by the process. What is seen as morally dangerous for the unwillingly unemployed person about to lose his home and car is seen as highly desirable for the corporation facing bankruptcy. Hell is paved with that kind of inconsistency.

For those who give aid, public projects may allow more effective discharge of a wider range of responsibilities. It was fitting for the good Samaritan to stop and provide limited personal aid to the neglected neighbor. For certain types of accident on a modern freeway, it is much more benevolent to speed past on the other side of the road to the nearest telephone and to summon the specialized services provided by modern government, such as radio-equipped police or emergency ambulances from public hospitals. Parents could express their responsibility for teaching their children by attempting daily lessons in the living room. Ordinarily it becomes a more serious acceptance of their parental obligation to pay school taxes, vote in school board elections, and join the parent-teacher association. In mass society, sensitivity to human need is often most effectively expressed through common action and specialized resources. In many of these instances the state becomes a tool for exercising responsibility and initiative. Genuine love often requires altered responses in the context of mass society and modern technology. To perpetuate expressions suitable to an unspecialized rural culture is actually to show less concern.

A second major test to apply to proposals for centralized planning is that of efficiency. Those who oppose extensions of planning are likely to suggest, for one thing, that mistakes of centralized planners will have a more widespread effect. Miscalculation or poor judgment with respect to national fiscal policy might, for example, intensify a recession over the entire economy. Admittedly this is true. It might be replied, however, that human fallibility operates without regard to the type of economy. The choice is not between fallible planners and infallible individual enterprisers. It can also be argued that overall planning bodies can have more of the essential data that are available than do competing businessmen who have more limited access to facts. The availability of more satisfactory indicators should also allow rapid readjustment when necessary.

Various limitations of the electorate are also held to be obstacles to democratic planning. Oscar Wilde once suggested that socialism would take too many evenings for meetings. Full participation by each citizen in every decision affecting his life would obviously be impossible, and besides, his input on technical matters would be disastrously mediocre. No political scientist would be so foolish as to propose such participation, and no citizen should be so masochistic as to desire it. The proper role of the citizenry in democratic decision is with regard to general policy. Detailed administration and day-to-day decisions are wisely left in the hands of specialists. The man on the street, given a decent education, is competent and has time to deal with general goals or directions for political and economic policy. It can be argued that involvement on the policy level by all citizens would lead to more enthusiastic support of adopted programs, thus contributing to greater efficiency. Or even if this were not so, the values of liberty might well be considered to outweigh those of somewhat extra efficiency.

The major objection here is to the inefficiencies of bureaucracy. Up to a point, increasing size of many types of organization can make for greater efficiency. An uncoordinated economy carries a heavy burden of duplication and waste. The same kind of efficiencies which planning produces in industries for private ends can also be realized for public ends, as in overall integration of road systems or the various elements in a fiscal policy. The losses due to corporate or government bureaucracy can be outweighed by the gains. There is, however, a limit to this. After a certain point, depending on the nature of the enterprise, units do become too large for maximum efficiency. Limits do need to be set to the comprehensiveness and centralization of any planning process. What this might mean with respect to government initiatives is discussed more specifically in a later section.

Efficiency in achieving certain ends of our society does now require some form of overall coordination. This is the only way to deal with some of our most important dilemmas, such as protection against the business cycle or maintenance of stability and growth in the total economy. The development of the American economy was always based on a combination of government and private enterprise. To the argument that "private enterprise built this country," one might ask what would have happened without land-grant colleges and county agents for agricultural improvement, grants of land to railroads, irrigation projects, and harbor development, to say nothing about consuls or protection against Hitlers abroad. These matters are frequently forgotten. People with strong private interests often have short historical memories. Now that we are taking seriously the distribution of abundance to the poor of the world, the prevention of war, or the solution of ecological problems, national policies become even more important. The unit for decision is inevitably larger as problems become more complex and comprehensive. Size is essential to certain purposes. If we insist on an economy of small units, such as is required for the market controls of a completely free enterprise system, "all that is necessary," as Galbraith has pointed out, "is to undo nearly everything that, at whatever violence to meaning, has been called progress in the last half century. There must be no thought of supersonic travel, or exploring the moon, and there will not be many automobiles." [1] As projects become more complicated and universal, like the preservation of peace or the termination of pollution, the coordination required goes beyond corporations to states or even to the United Nations. As Justice Holmes said, "When I pay taxes, I buy civilization."

A third major test to apply to proposals for centralized planning is that of freedom. One of the objections to any substantial economic intervention by government is that this would endanger freedom. One form that this argument takes was elaborated by Friedrich Hayek. He insisted that because of the multiplicity of possible choices, it is impossible for a society to agree upon economic ends. Yet such agreement would be necessary for any substantial planning. This would require the arbitrary choice by planners of a goal desired by one minority and its imposition upon all other minorities. Or, to put the argument in a slightly different form, no group will abandon its plan. When its proposed goals meet difficulty or opposition, it will seek new powers to deal with the hindrances rather than consent to alterations in the plan. [2]

This theory would have startling implications if it were applied to political life. If it is impossible for a society to agree upon economic ends, then it also must be impossible to agree upon complex political ends. Democracy then becomes an illusion. The only form of government possible becomes the arbitrary dictatorship of one political minority over all others. Happily, Hayek is mistaken at this point. We do have procedures in public discussion and decision-making for arriving at a reasonable consensus on exceedingly complex political policies. Furthermore, this dismal argument overlooks the possibilities of planning for variety, as we do for example in public recreational facilities. Neither is it necessary, having accepted some coercion, to degenerate into the ultimate terrors of totalitarianism. All political decision is a matter of saying, "Thus far and no farther." Heimann said that Hayek's theory was "like saying that the surgeon's knife cannot stop short of cutting the patient's throat. If the use of the surgeon's knife is certainly not without danger, its non-use is far more dangerous; it is fatal." [3]

Another reason given for contrasting freedom with government direction is the assertion that significant planning necessitates holding certain variables constant—notably consumer demand and the mobility of the labor force. It is argued that the only way to do this is to ration commodities and to draft workers, thus denying freedom of consumers and vocational choice. While comprehensive planning might proceed in this fashion, there are good economic reasons for maintaining that such measures are not necessary. Past experience or current consumer demand might be made the basis for production goals, and workers might be attracted to understaffed areas by the lure of increased wages. This does suggest certain safeguards if centralized economic direction is to remain democratic, a subject to which I will return later.

It is certainly true that any social regulation does reduce someone's individual liberty. License laws keep people out of an occupation for which they cannot qualify. Zoning laws limit what a man can do with his property. The lack of such regulations would also destroy the freedoms that come with protection against incompetent, unlicensed doctors or from a smelly chemical factory across one's back fence. Furthermore, strictures on liberty are constantly being imposed from nonpolitical sources. Competition is extremely coercive for the person who fails. Unemployment limits liberty of choice for many workers, as depressions do for many entrepreneurs. If we are genuinely interested in maximizing freedom, we will find the rule, "that government is best which governs the least," too narrow a definition. It is more adequate to say, "That total social system is best which coerces the least." If the latter goal is to be realized, there are times that the economic aspects of the social system need to be regulated by the political.

This is particularly clear when one recalls the positive as well as the negative meaning of liberty. To be free, a man needs opportunity as well as permission, the presence of concrete resources as well as the absence of restraining authorities. Poverty is also a form of bondage. Paying starvation wages is at least as coercive as is a minimum wage law. To quibble about the coercion in democratic planning and to overlook the disastrous consequences of continuing existing exploitation is to strain out gnats and swallow camels (Matt. 23:23-24). It is hazardous to concentrate both economic and political power in a single institution, especially when that institution is the state with its sovereign power. But it is also a threat to freedom to give too little power to the state.

Even in the negative sense of the absence of external restraint, planning can expand freedom. In unplanned situations, long lists of important economic decisions are now being made without the participation of those affected by them. Insofar as state control gives citizens something to say where previously they had nothing to say, this becomes a nation with more freedom for all. Until we speak through government, we have nothing effective to say about the racial policies of industry, or the price policies of monopoly, or the speed of eradication of poverty.

The analysis of the fallacy of anarchy in Chapter 3 might be repeated here. The laissez-faire attempt at eliminating external restraint is transformed into its opposite, autocracy, and maximum liberty can be secured only by democratic controls. The anarchist is typically unaware of his own tyranny, whether he be the smoker who insists upon a cigar in a crowded room, or a business enterpriser who fixes many restricting conditions on the lives of his employees. He is often blind to the meaning of shared decision. Sir Ernest Barker illustrated this when he objected to accepting government regulation in return for only a small share in setting government policy. He said, "I surrender all of myself—and I surrender it all to 999 others as well as myself; I only receive a fraction of the sovereignty of the community; and ultimately I must reflect that if I am the thousandth part of a tyrant, I am also the whole of a slave." [4] His eloquence is undeniable. But he underestimates both the extent to which men were slaves before democratic decision, and the extent to which allies agreeing with any one of us give us a great deal more power. Such proportional participation in a shared community is the maximum liberty available if we are concerned about the equal freedom of others.

This approach would reject a view of the state as a separate entity set over against the people. It would rather see the state as a whole population in common action. Instead of the Marxist view that the state is the executive committee of the dominant class, or the robber baron's view that the state is a device for plundering the public, or the classical laissez-faire view of the state as a relatively inactive umpire, we can now see the state as a responsible instrument of democratic power.

Selected controls are necessary for the fullest preservation of individual freedom. As Mannheim said, "The weakening and passing of controls also implies the weakening and passing of liberty." [5] This is similar to the statement of Pope John XXIII in his encyclical *Mater et magistra*. Having affirmed the primacy of private initiative, he went on to say, "Where, on the other hand, appropriate activity of the State is lacking or defective, commonwealths are apt to experience incurable disorders, and there occurs exploitation of the weak by the unscrupulous strong, who flourish, unfortunately, like cockle among the wheat, in all times and places." [6] Wisely selected government controls become enabling and liberating factors rather than prohibiting and constraining forces. Totalitarianism is less likely to come through such desirable extensions of state power than through the breakdown of government that results from too little action to solve basic problems. Especially in an intricate and interdependent social system, there are new possibilities for simultaneously realizing both freedom and control. Victor Obenhaus went so far as to conclude, "If Alexander Hamilton and Thomas Jefferson could witness what has occurred in their country a century and a half after their famous controversy over concentration of government power, they would be surprised to learn that each had won his point." [7]

PARAMETERS FOR PLANNING

Accomplishing this benign synthesis requires setting certain limitations to the planning process. In the first place, this assumes that planning will be done in a democratic society with its political bill of rights in healthy condition. Governments remain nontyrannical only insofar as they act by the consent of the governed and guarantee the full right of continuing dissent in public discussion.

An important counterpart to such political habits would be an economic bill of rights consistently observed in practice, if not written into a constitutional document. Two essential articles in such a declaration of policy would guarantee general freedom of consumer choice and of vocational choice.[8] Neither of these can be absolutized, since each limits the other, and since other values may become more compelling in times of grave emergency such as war. In general, however, it would become guiding policy to avoid rationing goods and drafting workers. Overall coordination would be restricted to the types of planning possible within these parameters.

Political control of economic affairs should also be decentralized as much as possible. According to the principle of subsidiarity, which has been prominent in Roman Catholic ethics, it is wrong both to transfer to larger collectivities functions that can be performed by subordinate bodies, and to expect subordinate groups to do what only the state can accomplish. So long as essential public purposes can be so realized, matters of purely local concern should be settled on the local level. Issues affecting only particular functional groups should be decided by those groups. In addition, of course, certain uniformities need to be established, not only on the national level but even on a world scale. This would apply, for example, to uses of the ocean floor or aspects of international trade and currency.[9] Yet much can be decentralized. The Tennessee Valley Authority illustrates possibilities here. Increased participation through trade unions, cooperative societies, professional associations, and educational or cultural organizations might contribute to the same end. All of these provide centers of independent initiative to balance centralized judgment.

Planning should be limited in degree and range. Even in those occasional situations suggesting direct government management, it is not always necessary to control entire industries. There are advantages in government activity as a yardstick in competition with similar private activity. Furthermore, in its regulatory functions government should not attempt to control all details. The prestigious London *Economist* once observed: "The state should seek its ends by trying to influence the economic weather, not by trying to ration raindrops. . . . To centralize decisions on matters of detail is to choke the system with paper and the citizen with frustrated rage." [10] Government activity, subject to the limitations here implied, would help to keep proliferating bureaucracy within bounds; at the same time it would make possible the achievement of important common purposes.

Four areas that are of widespread concern because of their unique characteristics make government action especially appropriate. These situations call for either regulatory laws, or framework planning that will shape the general economic environment (as by taxation or interest rates influencing the aggregate volume of employment, consumption, or investment), or in some cases direct management of government-owned enterprise.

The first area for government initiative includes those acts which if left unrestricted would allow the few to control the many. Our entire code of criminal law is directed toward this end. Among the most important services government provides is a considerable degree of personal safety. We come by this not only by enforcing laws but also by getting at causes of crime and (someday, we hope) by improved correctional facilities. New needs for protection against harm and serious injustice are constantly arising, as in the case of monopoly exploitation or racial discrimination. A second area includes social goals that we are unable to reach unless we all act together. Since fires have a habit of spreading, it is in the public interest that every individual subscribe to the fire department. Nor can we protect natural resources if some are free to rape the forests. The same thing is true where there are obvious economies in maintaining only a single system, as of water distribution lines or highways. On many matters of foreign policy we must act together if we are to act at all. Business cycles cannot be controlled without measures affecting the general economy. Or everyone in a sub-group may need to act together before they can act at all. We can scarcely expect one manufacturer to install expensive pollution control equipment unless all his competitors are required to incur the same cost.

A third area for state initiative includes those economic activities which go beyond the resources or interest of private enterprise. The amounts of capital required may be too large, or there may be no commensurate profits involved, or risks may be too great for traditional investment. Illustrations would include space exploration, river and harbor improvement, and forms of foreign aid programs, such as basic education, that do not bring negotiable economic returns. A fourth major type of common action is dealing with major economic hazards that may strike any person through no fault of his own. Of these hazards, the most frequently considered by policy makers have been unemployment, old age, death to the breadwinner, industrial accidents, sickness, and crop failure. For some of these there is a heavy collective responsibility. For none of these is the individual sufferer always completely responsible. General economic conditions are related to unemployment, and industrial policy can contribute to accidents or social conditions to epidemics. Wherever there is such collective involvement, we need to assume responsibility for our corporate acts. In simpler matters, when a boy breaks a window with his baseball, we expect him to ring the doorbell and arrange to pay. The same moral considerations now apply to an even longer list of basic types of social insecurity.

These are hazards concerning which we can pool our risks, roughly in the fashion of an insurance approach. We have provided some help of this kind for all the hazards listed above, through measures such as workmen's compensation or social security programs. The broadest lack of coverage is at the point of sickness, where we now provide for only part of the population. It is understandable that there should be heavy pressure for some form of national health insurance, which would apply the principle we are discussing to this hazard also. Some economic hazards not so frequently discussed might be added to the list. These might include recompense for those who are the victims of crime, war, or major natural disasters such as earthquakes.

Democratic action in none of these four areas needs to become seriously oppressive or inefficient or subject to any of the other criticisms directed against planning. On the contrary, wise action in these areas could contribute a great deal to the general goals we all share for the economy. It is easier to accept these statements when we recognize that a double goal always involves some adaptation or compromise. A rich, multifaceted life does not allow for glittering simplifications. It is right that we should want both a wide possibility of pluralism and also the gains that require unity. It then becomes necessary that we understand the requirements for the combination. If a husband and wife want both a tasty meal and togetherness, each can order a personal preference from the menu, but both have to go to the same restaurant. The four categories just discussed help to draw the line between social control and individual freedom in such a way as to maintain as much as possible of both harmony and variety.

AGENDA FOR ACTION

Yet something more than a list of general categories is necessary for that kind of symphonic orchestration. More specifically, what items are urgently required on our agenda as priorities for the next decade? What balance of public and private initiative is called for to deal with them? In the first chapter of this book, major ethical guidelines were elaborated as guides to our social priorities. These included human fulfillment, equal opportunity, maximization of liberty, and supportive, dynamic community. If we take these seriously, our agenda will include at least the following items.[11]

1. We need to improve our protection of the general conditions necessary for maintaining a healthy economy. While government planning (plus war) has already safeguarded us against any recent major depression, cyclical recessions have brought unacceptable rates of unemployment and unnecessary retardation of economic growth. Continuing inflation has brought hardships, especially to fixed-income people, and has bedeviled our attempts at full employment. Yet we have at hand devices for modifying even more beneficially the framework within which private business decisions are made. These devices include monetary and fiscal, taxation, and public services policies. For example, interest rates can be lowered to stimulate economic activity or raised to retard investment. Or, by undertaking more public services programs during a period of recession, the government might do more to create jobs. (One of the grave inconsistencies of our times is that those who object to the government's becoming the employer of last resort are quite willing to have the government become the employer of first resort for young men drafted into the military, even though the latter involves

a degree of compulsion that we ought to oppose for government employment in general.)

2. Existing poverty and inequality urgently demand attention. The ethics of inequality discussed earlier focuses a powerful spotlight on the social sin of undeserved hunger in an affluent society. Even more than a private tragedy, this becomes a public crime. Insofar as we are sensitive to need, we will build a floor below which no person will fall as long as he is willing to make a social contribution. A program to implement this will have several aspects.

A basic approach to the relief of poverty is through the extension of economic opportunity. This implies all that has just been said about the general health of the economy. It presupposes also the elimination of all discrimination on the grounds of race or sex or class. It suggests a role for labor unions in defending the legitimate rights of workers, and for government in keeping minimum wage rates as high as economically feasible. When people get excited about the "welfare mess" they need to be reminded that full employment at decent wages is a good place to start welfare reform. However, since such large numbers of people on welfare (such as the aged or the handicapped) are unemployable, this alone will not be enough. A second and closely related essential is the casework approach. Since numerous persons have unique combinations of obstacles to adequate self-support, a variety of individualized programs are called for, including career counseling, education or retraining, and referral to specialized agencies. Those who argue that a guarantee of a very minimal income, as in the negative income tax, could eliminate all the expenses of social work, are neglecting the complex variety of human need.

The productivity approach is a third instrument for the alleviation of poverty. Improved methods produce a bigger stockpile to be divided. Conservatives are right in insisting that we cannot distribute what we do not have. It would obviously help if we sharply reduced the wastes of inefficiency, planned obsolescence, and war. Even a modest reduction in military expenditures would make available vast amounts for other human needs. Improving industrial productivity is also to a great extent a matter for private business. A key question concerns the willingness of business leaders to share larger portions of increased productivity with workers, keeping smaller portions for high-income groups or for unnecessary expansion into gadgets for the affluent instead of essentials for the poor.

The redistribution approach provides a fourth instrument for the alleviation of poverty. This becomes particularly important insofar as we recognize that the degree of inequality is itself a problem, and that too-great riches also create an ethical handicap. From this point of view it makes sense to establish a less elastic ceiling for top incomes at the same time as we provide a rising floor for low incomes.[12] Social invention has provided us with new methods for distributive justice which were unknown in former days. Many of them can be summed up in the phrase "progressive taxation and regressive social services." In income tax schedules we tax higher incomes at a progressively higher rate, with the theoretical possibility of taking all additional income beyond a stated figure. At the same time society provides free or low-cost services of a type that are a greater help to the poor than to the rich. Free public education or parks or low-cost housing are especially helpful to the poor, since the rich could easily send their children to college or picnic at the country club or rent an apartment anyway. Such redistribution of economic power is what the world economic revolution is all about. We can try to obstruct it, but only at the cost of moral death and worldwide social explosion.

In relieving poverty there is now some tendency to move from a services strategy to an income strategy, in such a proposal as a guaranteed annual income, a negative income tax (with those below a specified level receiving money from the Internal Revenue Service instead of paying in), or family assistance programs. In effect, we already have what might be labeled a modest guaranteed survival income. Our society does not knowingly permit any person completely to starve. Guaranteed minimal income proposals have several advantages over present welfare practices. They could be less paternalistic in allowing the recipient himself to decide how to spend his income. Well-planned programs could be less expensive. Some current programs for warring on poverty are scandalously wasteful. Not a high enough percentage of amounts appropriated actually gets to the poor. Adequate annual income proposals could also raise the amounts available to those in lower-income brackets by larger amounts than we have been willing to put into our present programs. Without our going into all the arguments pro and con,[13] it should be pointed out that such proposals could be drafted so as to provide incentives to work by allowing recipients to keep a portion of their earnings. Even a conservative economist like Friedman recognizes the incentives objection to be a fallacy and advocates a negative income tax.[14]

3. Major modern needs include supplementary services that often benefit all citizens, such as improved housing, education, transportation, and medical care. The impact of blighted housing is spread through entire cities. Public education needs improvement in all parts of the country. Efficient, low-cost mass transportation is becoming more important in view of ecological factors that threaten us all. Not only the poor but also families of moderate means can be bankrupted by catastrophic illness. These needs have been so widely discussed elsewhere that it is not necessary here to recapitulate detailed arguments. A strong case can be made for improving or extending available services in all these areas.

Here again conclusions are strongly affected by ethical commitments. To which needs are our overall policies to be directed—those of the rich or of the poor? Or to put this in another way, how deeply do we make the claim of the most needy a directive for ourselves? A clear conclusion of an ethics of love is that the most needy should have priority. According to classical marginal utility theory, resources should be employed at that point which brings the highest return per unit of investment. Morality insists that utility be defined in human terms to an even greater extent than in terms of monetary profit. Our attention is then first of all directed toward those whose opportunities for housing, education, transportation, and medical care are the poorest.

4. The items thus far listed on a contemporary agenda have dealt chiefly with providing opportunity through better production and distribution. There are also items primarily related to freedom in the sense of the absence of restraint. One of these is the control of gigantic business units tending toward monopoly. These become threats to liberty insofar as they are able to decide what is to be produced, to administer prices to the point of greatest profitability, and to manipulate consumer wants through advertising. Citizens have no direct control over giant corporations, which may constitute a larger operation than many nations and which in their multinational form may control the political policies of many states.

Private control of such vast power cannot be tolerated. Society might handle this problem by choosing from among at least five different approaches. As it was pointed out in Chapter 3, large-scale enterprise may result in efficiencies as well as in dangers. One possibility is that, because we want the efficiencies, we may permit corporations to grow to a larger size than we have been willing to tolerate in the past. Or, in cases that we consider particularly dangerous, we may "bust the trusts" into smaller units. A third possibility is the kind of gentle influence that might be exerted by public members on boards of directors or by advisory committees of public-spirited citizens, along with public exposure of policies that such representatives considered socially detrimental. Or we might move to regulate certain large enterprises, as we do the so-called natural monopolies, such as telephone or electric service. This may break down because of the great complexity and expense of securing accurate information or because the regulated so easily become the regulators. In this case, a fifth possible policy, presumably held as a last resort, becomes social ownership. Either the industry might be entirely socialized, making possible some indirect control of policy by the population as a whole, or the government might manage one company in the industry in competition with other privately owned enterprises.

Another current need is eliminating the disproportionate political power of a few and providing such extensions of participatory democracy as will guarantee an equally effective vote to each citizen. Government can protect constitutional provisions by safeguarding the integrity of the election process, or by controlling disproportionate campaign spending, or by insuring equal-sized constituencies for representation in legislative bodies. Political parties bear a heavy responsibility for responsive internal decision-making processes, and for terminating the antiquated seniority system for congressional leadership. Citizens need to use the rights they have, including active participation in politics, in interest groups, or in community organization. Eternal vigilance by the public is still the price of liberty.

One important aspect of freedom is the protection of the right of labor as well as of management to organize for collective bargaining and social action. This right will be further discussed later in this chapter. There is one related issue that may here be raised since it affects the liberties of everybody— namely, labor's right to strike and the corresponding coercive powers of management. At the moment, the right to strike is vital to organized workers. It is necessary to maintain that balance of power which is essential to genuine negotiation. Simply to leave the discussion at that point, however, is no longer adequate to current needs. Massive coercive methods in industrial relations, whether used by management or labor, constitute a primitive procedure. Strikes, for example, are damaging to laborers' wages and to management's profits, while the general public is caught in the cross fire with losses of products and services. Particularly in industries vital to the total economy or to the public health or safety, the freedom of the people as a whole demands such possible alternatives as voluntary arbitration, mediation, and continuous negotiation. Since increasingly the public interest is affected by wage and profit patterns, the extension of freedom itself may require in the most threatening cases some form of compulsory decision, perhaps in a system of specialized labor courts. Such decisions would be made in accord with overall guidelines established through democratic processes, and they would be equally binding on employers. If workers in vital industries are not to be allowed to strike, management cannot be allowed unilaterally to impose on labor its decisions in matters that are appropriate for collective bargaining.

5. Beyond questions of freedom, other immediate concerns relate to the quality or even survival of community. Ecological considerations have recently catapulted toward the top of our list of priorities, propelled to this kind of "best seller" rating by the obvious plight of modern cities. It is no cause for pride to hear the predictions of futurologists about gargantuan megalopolises that might be called "Boswash" (stretching from Boston to Washington) or "Chipitts" (Chicago to Pittsburgh), or "Sansan" (San Diego to San Francisco).[15] A great deal of manpower needs to be thrown into the rebuilding and regoverning of cities or into the design of new, decentralized centers of population.

Pollution is extending from the noise and dirt and lethal gases of the city to infest the rivers, lakes, fields, and atmosphere of the countryside. Unless this is stemmed, the earth may not remain habitable. Basic natural resources are becoming depleted through competitive exploitation for bombs and gadgets by larger populations with so-called higher standards of living. All these problems are intensified by a runaway increase in population that not only fills space but uses up resources and litters its wastes.

A pluralistic mix is as appropriate for dealing with this complex of difficulties as it was for other items on our agenda. A great deal can be done by private enterprises. Government cannot escape responsibility for conservation laws, planning for urban renewal, and regulating pollution. Crowding masses into limited spaces with scarce resources always requires social planning. It was not necessary for government regulation to apply to redwood trees, or to windmills in Holland, until they began to disappear.

6. When economic agenda are listed, an item often neglected is the redefinition of our standard of living. The 6 percent of the world's population that lives in the United States cannot continue to use up 40 percent of the world's natural resources without disaster. To reduce or to shift production is a major undertaking, at least comparable to economic adjustments following a major war. Nevertheless, with firm alacrity, we need to transfer resources from comparatively frivolous uses in overdeveloped countries to supplying stark necessities in underdeveloped countries. Increasing some items in the gross national product will become counterproductive. There are electrical novelties that we do not need and should refuse to buy. The defeat of further national funds for the development of the supersonic transport may mark the beginning of public wisdom and the recognition that more and "better" ecological monstrosities can only carry us back to the Stone Age.

The most constructive progress now requires our willingness to pay taxes to be used for the benefit of those who are poorer than we are, both at home and abroad. It is impossible to find cheap solutions to expensive problems. In making ghettos livable there is no substitute for taxation. Speeches by the mayor do not fulfill the same function as parks or efficient mass transit systems. It is true that ending poverty and achieving full employment would add enough to the national product so that even the same tax rate would yield a considerably larger revenue. As Michael Harrington has suggested, "Justice would, so to speak, finance itself." [16] Nevertheless, justice requires as great a willingness to be taxed to eliminate poverty as to maintain defense expenditures or assorted projects to help the wealthier. One of the most dependable of public reactions is pressure to keep taxes down. But this attempt to reduce our tax burden while millions suffer in ways that could be relieved by those tax funds, is one of the most immoral aspects of all our prevailing folk wisdom. From the Judeo-Christian perspective one may argue the details about what taxes are to be used for, but the necessity for sharing is not up for debate.

This shift in emphasis is partly a matter of personal values. Harvey Cox described as "technological asceticism" his family's somewhat extreme experiment in getting along without telephone, television, and other impediments of the American "good life." [17] Dealing with the larger problem is also a matter of corporation policy, investors' judgment, and social planning. The emphasis on redefinition suggests shifting a larger proportion of total production to a different kind of product. The gross national product would still be expected to increase, but it would be directed more largely toward a new quality of life. Instead of a higher standard of living achieved through larger quantities of the same values, a higher quality of life is now to be experienced by adding more levels of values. The economy is to be directed less toward maximum material production and more toward a new preoccupation that moves beyond the sensate and the secular. The coming life-style will reject more luxurious homes, bigger cars, faster jet planes, and overkill military capacity, recognizing that our most important problems are much deeper than the problems these can touch. A shining new camper beside a polluted stream does not make much sense, nor does a luxuriously furnished home plus an empty mind and a homeless spirit. More and more traditional goods will get us into deeper trouble internationally, ecologically, and morally. Opportunity now consists of a more modest material style of life, combined with a richer social and spiritual standard of living. The society of the future will undoubtedly relate production and politics more closely. Will it also add poetry and prayer? Will the products of productive skill increasingly sustain the solution of major social problems, the cultivation of resources in group relationships, and the release of the intellectual, aesthetic, moral, and religious capacities of man?

These are values that do not unduly exhaust physical resources nor pollute the atmosphere. They are also enterprises in which the public sector of the economy and private non-profit agencies would play a larger part, at least in the initial stages. Presumably government on various levels would need to make provision for more extensive adult education, personal-growth clinics, livelihood for artists and musicians, low-cost travel opportunities, folk-art galleries in every neighborhood, or traveling drama productions reaching isolated towns. In view of the separation of church and state, churches would need to provide for new religious explorations. They might be joined by welfare agencies in moving beyond delinquency or marriage counseling to career counseling, ethical consultation, and spiritual life direction. Conceivably some of these might develop into professions to be practiced privately for fees. Private foundations or pressure groups might employ more social activists working on poverty, war, or race. In getting such novel vocations off the ground, initiative and financial support would have to come from nonbusiness sources. As one economist has put it, "the thing at which businessmen are best—the production and sale of marketable goods and services—is no longer the thing that stands at the head of America's list of needs." [18] Our propensity to neglect the public sector and to concentrate on developing the private sector of the economy creates an increasingly serious imbalance as we move into a more creative future.

If we see the creation of a new post-industrial culture as one of our chief orders of business, other basic features of a capitalist society also become less appropriate. We will then be dealing to a greater extent with abundant values (such as insights, which are multiplied as they are shared) rather than with scarce values (such as money, which is diminished as it is divided). Under such circumstances, competition for getting ahead will have less meaning. The incentive of material acquisition will become less important. Many of the professional services to be rendered, from the medical to the religious, would be corrupted to the extent that the profit motive entered in. The goods most cherished will not be those that can be privately owned. One cannot claim ownership of an idea, nor sell two square inches of an appreciation. All this enhances the possibilities for a gentler, more cooperative society, purposefully aiming at common nonmaterial goals. Thirty years ago Edward H. Carr, a British professor of international politics, spoke of a coming age in which the welfare of individuals would be regarded as a problem for society as a whole, and in which the quantitative concept of wealth as the end of economic activity would be discarded in favor of the qualitative conception of welfare. He pointed out that it is no longer possible to identify what is socially desirable with what "pays," and he said, "It is clear that the regulating force of the economic system under which we live must more and more be sought in the realm of ethics rather than in the operations of a price mechanism." [19]

This is not to negate what has been said previously about technological necessities and continued production of material goods for human needs, but it is to place this in a new setting. It is to recognize that adequate agendas for the future will be not palliative but profound, or revolutionary, in the sense that basic and rapid (though nonviolent) changes must take place. They push outward to a genuine redistribution of wealth and power, resulting in greater economic equality and political participation. They also push upward to a new quality of life.

Formula for Pluralism

The previous sections have illustrated the variety of ways for meeting high-priority problems. In some cases individual or corporate approaches are most effective. In other cases social planning is called for. To rely on one where the other is essential becomes disastrous. To insist on a false uniformity is to take on an unnecessary handicap. Ours has become and should continue to remain a mixed economy, or pluralist society. This concept introduces into economic structure principles that have long been a part of our political practice, principles such as divided authority, a variety of power blocs, and effective checks and balances. As used with reference to economic systems, the concept of a mixed economy usually refers to a blend of capitalist, socialist, and consumer-cooperative elements. The term therefore has an elastic meaning, since it allows for blending these elements in considerably different proportions. The possible value of such a system is that it might combine the best of all possible worlds in a creative synthesis, securing values that would otherwise be lost. It might, for example, allow social policies contributing to economic growth, without choking the political process with bureaucratic detail. The danger is that unwise combination might secure the worst of all possible worlds—for example, by reducing incentive without securing the full efficiency of planning. All economies have been mixed to a certain extent. There were some state controls even in the most extreme laissez-faire capitalisms. There is some private ownership in communist societies. We are moving into a more balanced combination that gives a distinctive meaning to the term. Even now, however, the issue still remains as to the proportions in which various ingredients are to be mixed.

The directions for change that have heretofore been outlined would leave most economic activity in private hands. Consumer goods would overwhelmingly be so owned and controlled. Individuals could buy fattening potato chips or slimming celery according to personal preference, since it is hard to see how such choices could in any way harm their neighbors. Most business and professional activities would be conducted by individuals, partnerships, or corporations. The state would not interfere with acts having only unimportant social consequences. When the democratic state did take initiative it would do so only with majority support and with full rights to civil liberties for minorities protected. We are recognizing the possibility of even wider varieties of pluralism than had once been acceptable—as in styles of dress or personal appearance, in certain private sexual practices, or in exempting sincere conscientious objectors from universally required government action, such as the military. So long as there are no serious social consequences, acts that are personally harmful call for moral education but not for government regulation.

The necessities for regulatory action by government are reduced to the extent that private business is beginning to adopt ethical standards that are more socially responsible.[20] Increasingly, business leaders are accepting labor participation in collective bargaining on a longer list of issues of concern to workers. Corporations have introduced ombudsmen as people's representatives. There is wider recognition that business has an obligation to attack a broad range of social problems, working toward employment for minorities, reduced pollution, improved television programs, or safer products, even at the risk of some reduction of profits. A substantial segment of the business community may yet come to see that the business of business is no longer merely to increase conventional productivity but to improve social justice and the quality of life.

The market mechanism is still extremely valuable for registering a wide variety of complex preferences. Even communist nations have moved to a somewhat larger reliance upon this aspect of the price system. Munby calls the market mechanism "one of the most useful achievements of human inventiveness." He then also adds, "The mechanism is not one suitable for dealing with all human problems; it has distinct limitations even within its special field, and as a whole it has to be subjected to political control." [21] As a decidedly more conservative economist, Friedman would considerably limit the range of government activity. Nevertheless he also sees the necessity for some state economic decisions where a single overall policy is essential. He says, "It is precisely the existence of such indivisible matters . . . that prevents exclusive reliance on individual action through the market." [22]

In some respects economic activity by the state can be sharply reduced, as in excessive military expenditures, anachronistic projects, and unnecessary bureaucratic proliferation. Furthermore, there can be a considerable amount of pluralism in government activity. Decisions with only local consequence should be locally made. This includes matters such as city planning and many aspects of school administration. Or, a great deal is to be said for various types of regulation or for semiautonomous public corporations, instead of direct government management, for some purposes.

When all this has been said, citizens will also have to perform certain functions through the state. For reasons elaborated in previous chapters, we will need to continue to use government for some of our major economic needs, such as handling monopoly, major economic hazards, high-capital or low-profit activities, or projects in which the public interest is dominant. If we expect to eliminate poverty, improve the environment, and move toward a higher order of existence, we can scarcely do so without the full initiative of responsible government. In a properly mixed economy we need to leave the market to do what it can still do, but we need to supplement it through government activity. With respect to any specific function, we will need to draw up a balance sheet of outcomes and decide what is needed in the light of the unique characteristics of that particular situation. The promise of a properly mixed economy is that there shall be a large enough government sector to provide its indispensable benefits and a large enough private sector to prevent insufferable centralization.

In addition to private and government enterprise, consumers' cooperatives provide a third type of economic structure, to an even greater extent in some other countries than in the United States. When twenty-eight weavers in Rochdale, England, opened their store on the fourth day before Christmas, 1844, they introduced a distinctive emphasis into the world of commerce. Each of the poverty-stricken members had pledged two pence per week toward what finally became a meager stock of flour, oatmeal, butter, and sugar. From these beginnings grew the British cooperative movement, which grew to be one of the largest distribution systems in the domestic commerce of England.

The distinguishing features of cooperatives can be described in the Rochdale principles, which are generally accepted by the worldwide movement.[23] The first of these principles is open membership. Any person can join a cooperative without distinction as to race, politics, religion, or wealth. This is in contrast to corporations, which sell stock only to those with enough capital to invest. (Credit unions are an exception here. Both by legal enactment and for sound practice, the requirement of a common bond among members seems desirable when one makes loans.) A second principle is returning a limited interest on capital invested rather than paying investors a fluctuating share of the profits. A third distinctive feature is democratic control. In what cooperators refer to as the primacy of people, each member has one vote for the board of directors and on general policies. In other business corporations some members vote considerably more often, once for each share of voting stock they own or can gather a proxy for. A fourth practice is the return of net earnings in refunds to patrons in proportion to the amount of their patronage, rather than the traditional corporation's distribution of surplus to shareholders in proportion to their investment. Prime Minister William Ewart Gladstone considered that "the cooperative concept of the patronage refund is the greatest economic discovery of the nineteenth century." A fifth general principle is cooperation among cooperatives, including federation wherever possible for mutual support, to this extent substituting cooperation for competition. For example, retail cooperatives organize cooperative wholesales which then undertake manufacturing.

Cooperatives have become a way in which little people can own big things, which are operated to serve the needs of users instead of the profits of owners. Consumer control can be extended over a nationwide or even a worldwide coordinated network, and yet participation can be decentralized to a local neighborhood outlet. This provides a means to nourish democracy at the grass roots instead of allowing too-great centralization. In addition to wholesale and retail distribution of a wide variety of commodities, cooperatives have also been organized for housing, burial, medical care, insurance, power distribution, and the marketing of agricultural products. Most familiar to urban Americans probably are credit unions, which are consumers' cooperatives providing certain banking services.

Besides consumers' cooperatives, other functional groups provide important centers for economic decision in a pluralistic society. They also stand between the individual and the state, or act as a check or balancing force on other powerful groups. One such major interest group is organized labor, which protects workers' interests by pressure on government and acts as a balancing force over against organized management.[24] The organized labor movement remains essential, for an individual workingman cannot hope to match the bargaining strength of a corporation. Given men as they are, justice is more likely to be approximated if parties come into negotiations with more equal strength. Labor's right to organize and bargain collectively must be protected if we take economic aims of freedom and equal opportunity seriously. The existence of such countervailing forces as organized labor and management strengthens the possibility for self-regulation within the economy and lessens the need for more detailed government controls.

Organized labor has come a long way since its early experiences of facing goon squads or court injunctions or the National Guard. It has won a large measure of participatory democracy and has supported a long list of forward-looking social changes. It still remains an important source of support for progressive change on specific issues such as health insurance or certain aspects of civil rights. It provides a counterforce against the pretensions and biases of capital. Yet, as do all human groups, a successful labor movement is developing its own set of egoistic pretensions and biases. When the salaries voted union officers begin to imitate those of high corporation officials, labor loses a good deal of its moral authority. Like other formerly liberal movements in a dynamic period of history, organized labor is becoming too much a conservative force. It seems no longer eager to organize those at the bottom of the economic ladder, and it does not seem to be vigorously campaigning about very many reforms. There are exceptions to this, as in the case of César Chavez and the farm workers. On the whole, in basically improving international relations, in challenging materialistic life-styles, and in supporting the interests of the Third World, organized labor has too often taken a *status quo* position.

The kind of dynamic pluralism outlined in this chapter is supported by sophisticated ethical analysis. Moral guidelines are always to be related to the varied and complex situations in which action actually occurs. Differing circumstances call for different decisions if the same system of values is to be most fully realized. The thoroughly loving parent deals with each child somewhat differently because each is a unique individual. Economic and political forms should likewise be expected to differ wherever the nature of the situation is significantly different. For this reason economic analysis and political analysis are a necessary part of ethical analysis. Only so can we understand the distinctive nature of specific situations, the alternative choices actually available, and the probable consequences of each. Only with this degree of understanding can we relate values and goals to the full range of basic decisions to be made.

The ethical thrust also accelerates dynamic movement within each aspect of the complex whole. Our generation faces the broad agenda of a pluralistic society with the genuine possibility of a radically new interpretation of the good life and the emergence of human potentialities never before experienced in history. These unprecedented possibilities require rejection of much in our commonly accepted ethos. Such a transformation is inconceivable without the resurgence of a more demanding morality and the empowerment of what Harrington called "the conscience constituency." [25]

In listing the values to be actualized, an adequate ethic moves through a hierarchy of values from the material at the bottom through the social in the intermediate position to the spiritual (intellectual, moral, aesthetic, and religious) at the top. In defining for whom these values are to be sought, an adequate morality moves from the self out to others. With respect to the element of time, movement is from the short run to the long run. In each of these three dimensions the maturely moral man seeks the full range of possibilities, including material, social, and spiritual, for both self and others over the full range of time. But in a finite situation such inclusive realization becomes impossible and a choice must be made. Wherever a conflict develops, it is the latter end of the continuum, i.e., higher values for others in the long run, that is to be given priority. This is the reverse of the emphasis of much of prevailing culture. Another important insight from our Judeo-Christian heritage is that unless the latter ends of the three continua are given priority, the first ends cannot be sustained or fully realized. This is to say that our contemporary reversal of priorities shuts the door to the possibility of actualizing the full range of value. Materialism, egoism, and immediacy are all self-defeating.

Furthermore, the meaning of the latter or priority terms in each of the three dimensions is enhanced by religious dedication. Spiritual values come to include the meaning of the whole and of the ultimate in reality and God. This makes a considerable difference in the completeness of human actualization. Lopping off the highest ranges keeps our expectations more completely contented with the mediocre and the partial. It omits the possibility of relationship to God and growing likeness to his perfection. Lengthening the self-neighbor continuum includes within the circle of love the most distant of persons and calls for a more active and sacrificial response to the total needs of all men, including enemies. This pushes us beyond parochialism or the common decencies of the suburbanite. Extending the time dimension includes in ethical decision not only all future generations but the mystery of eternity. We then see ourselves as knit together in the fabric of all those who will ever live and who by their interdependence shape to some slight but significant degree the nature of the continuing universe. Any blight on personality then becomes even more atrociously wrong. Imperialism and racism not only have consequences for our children and grandchildren, but, in ways not completely understood, they decrease the sum total of deposits of good will in the total universe for all time.

In short, the absence of a transcendent dimension truncates our norms and expectations. Such a beheaded morality can become economically and politically, as well as personally, devastating. Decapitation of aspirations reduces dissonance and thereby invites disaster. Including the full range of theological considerations, on the other hand, allows a sounder and sturdier thrust into the future. Anyone who accepts this kind of religion or ethics cannot avoid commitment to comprehensive change, including root motivations and causes. The only time a Christian can be a conservative is when, after thorough investigation, he cannot possibly find anything better to do than is now being done.

In the Bible, God is always doing things that are utterly new and unprecedented. He creates a universe and then man. He sees people through an exodus and into a promised land. He said, through Isaiah: "Behold I am doing a new thing. . . . I will make a way in the wilderness and rivers in the desert" (Isa. 43:19). He makes men new beings in Christ (II Cor. 5:17) and is somehow creating "new heavens and a new earth" so absorbing that "former things shall not be remembered" (Isa. 65:17; compare II Peter 3:13, Rev. 21:1, 5).

Deeply motivated religious persons will work not only at basic and thoroughgoing change but also at rapid transformation. A holy impatience results from realization of how diabolical existing evil is and how much every man now living deserves access to God-given resources he does not now have. This is a stentorian summons that allows neither negligence nor delay. God's creative energies continue to move to make all things new, and no person realizes his individual destiny until he becomes immersed in that creative process.

5
STRATEGIES
AND LIFE-STYLES

THE BEST SYSTEM that inspired human brains can devise still relieves no poverty so long as the plan exists only on paper. Moving toward an acceptable economic future involves not only describing adequate ends but also implementing effective means. These two go together like car and gasoline, or speaker and voice. Goals without methods for reaching them are as helpless as a Scrabble player holding a Q without a U. Yet, choosing methods to gain objectives stirs up all kinds of ethical as well as practical problems. Winston Churchill during World War II was asked how he could reconcile his democratic goals with supporting his Soviet allies. He is reported to have replied: "I have only one purpose, the destruction of Hitler, and my life is much simplified thereby. If Hitler invaded Hell I would make at least a favorable reference to the Devil in the House of Commons." [1] As Churchill himself knew, such problems cannot be simplified quite so easily.

Ethical insight insists that means and ends are closely related, and that both must be carefully evaluated. Since ends are impossible without means, mistaken strategies weaken one's own cause. They become one way of comparatively strengthening the opposition. Not doing all that we could have done is one way of throwing the game to the opponent. Furthermore, the means always color and may even completely alter the ends attained. Many who have discarded their illusions about existing structures still cling to illusions about the way to change those structures. Utopianism is as devastating in the one case as in the other. Oversimplifiers are so impressed by some aspects of the situation that they overlook even more important factors. This is like knowing that one starts a car by letting out the clutch and forgetting that one must also start the motor. In a flight from reality, the oversimplifier is too-little informed by history and the full range of contemporary data. His conclusions grow out of a dream world instead of an authentic vision. An indictment is not a strategy. Successful revolution requires more than a collage of slogans.

The abolition of poverty, redistribution of wealth and power, and shifts to new preoccupations with previously neglected values will not come easily. Powerful interests offer gigantic resistance. In a society dominated by large units, it is questionable whether the people can still shape public decision. Where is countervailing power to be found against the military-industrial complex? What strategies of intervention are both ethically defensible and socially effective?

The Politics of Polarization and Domination

This particular strategy is a standard reliance for radicals at both left and right extremes of the opinion spectrum. Both groups are very deeply convinced of the correctness of their own position. At the same time they have met seemingly unyielding opposition from almost everybody. Therefore they understandably conclude that the usual methods of education, discussion, and persuasion will not work to produce the basic, rapid change they consider necessary. Instead of playing such futile verbal games, they push beyond customary forms of dissent to more militant protest, and from protest to disruption of the normal activities of established institutions. They expect that this will create confrontations during which their opponents will overreact. As the police begin mercilessly to club those who have occupied a building or a park, more persons will view sympathetically the cause of the demonstrators. According to leftist expectations, the establishment will be shown up for the suppressive monstrosity they consider it to be. Rightists expect communists, or closely related radicals, to show themselves in their true and despicable colors. In both cases it is anticipated that this strategy will radicalize potential allies and polarize the population. Those closest to the campaigning group will join it, while those with strong predispositions toward the opposition will move into its orbit.

One result will be to weaken, fragment, and immobilize the moderate center, which both groups consider to be their chief competitor. Fewer persons will be willing to support modest reform measures. Indeed, in the growing confusion and threat, there will be a fragmentation of the center into many helpless, competing splinter groups. This is a prelude to chaos, with a nation coming apart at the seams. Disruption and widespread opposition will make it impossible for existing leadership to govern. The functioning of established institutions will break down, leaving the field to the radicals at both extremes. In the ensuing sharp conflict, strategists of this stripe expect to win and to impose a new order. While it is not always openly admitted, a victory violently won by a minority must be maintained by a dictatorship of the victor.

When any group feels deeply disturbed about injustice and frustrated about change, it more easily accepts such violent and authoritarian strategies. The transformation of the egalitarian into the elitist is terrifying to behold. On the other hand, comfortable beneficiaries of iniquitous circumstances easily become self-righteous in their criticism, especially if they themselves are doing nothing significant to remove the injustice. While avoiding this kind of insensitivity and arrogance, it is still important to point out grave defects in polarization strategies, particularly when these obstruct the very justice they are designed to attain.

One difficulty is that such strategies strengthen the opposition by creating a powerful backlash. The political strength of

Ronald Reagan and George Wallace is to a considerable extent due to campus turmoil and urban terrorism. Steven Kelman saw that disorders such as those at Harvard led to a counter-attack by voters, who took their revenge on election day. He wrote: "While Harvard awaits the revolution, black people in the ghettos, the poor in Appalachia, the farm worker in California, experiences the counter-revolution. . . . My bitterness comes from the unhappy realization that many of the people I know at school have become part of the problem." [2] The social reformer always needs to multiply and solidify his own support and to divide his opposition. Given the negative attitude toward disruption and violence in modern American culture, resort to such tactics is likely to do just the opposite, to divide one's supporters and to multiply and solidify the opposition. Advocates of polarization have no need to deny the strengthening of the opposition, for indeed it is part of what their theory anticipated. What leftist radicals overlook is that when it comes to a showdown, repression and reaction are more likely to win, given the present distribution of force in the United States. Their efforts will actually have contributed to an American type of fascism. This kind of program is self-contradictory. It is like a man so desperately wanting to get to Paris quickly that he begins by burning all airplanes, boats, and spaceships, and shooting all horses.

Changes of the magnitude now needed in the United States will not be won without aggressive and powerful demands. Neither will they be won by unnecessarily building up a strong backlash. There is research evidence to show that measured threat may motivate to constructive action. A threat that is too great, on the other hand, has the opposite effect.[3] From a sociological approach, Allen D. Grimshaw has pointed out that if society at large identifies a method of change as a legitimate protest against unjust conditions, people will be more disposed to accept constructive changes. If, however, accepted cultural definitions label the methods used as "criminal" or "rebellious," then the choice before the people is weighted in such a way that their already great tendency to opt for reactionary repression is strengthened.[4] If those advocating change cut themselves off from the overwhelming majority of the population and from communication with large membership organizations, they give up the possibility of ever winning majority support for their program. That is, they give up the possibility of democratic change.

This problem becomes particularly acute when violence becomes a part of the method used. From an ethical standpoint it must be admitted that there can be a just revolution of a violent type. If there is no other way to gain justice, and if in the total outcome gains outweigh losses, it may be preferable to choose limited revolutionary violence in preference to a continuation of serious systemic violence continuously being practiced as a part of existing culture. Men are now dying just as surely from too little food and medical attention as they would from a bullet wound. A person loses his house if a violent man burns it down. He loses it just as surely if a racist discriminates against him by discharging him from his job with the result that he cannot keep up his payments. It might be argued, in fact, that there are advantages to murder, because there is less prolonged pain, and to burning a house, because the victim can at least collect the fire insurance! [5]

The very fact that there is so much existing violence becomes a strong argument for the most rapid change possible. However, in actuality this becomes a telling argument *against* revolutionary violence, since in our circumstances it is counterproductive and is likely to lead to the opposite results from those intended. Regardless of what may be said about other countries, in the United States a violent strategy makes victory less likely. Furthermore, in all situations violent victory tends to result in many of the same evils against which it was directed, such as dictatorship, class domination, and imperialism. Russia and other communist countries illustrate the fact that to a significant degree revolutionaries become like what they overthrow. The means tend to corrupt the end. Between evenly matched adversaries, where each can throw in additional forces to stave off defeat, the consequences of violence become cumulative in a vicious circle of reprisals. In a complex industrial civilization violent strategies become even more widely destructive in their secondary effects. Guerrilla warfare in the streets of modern New York or Chicago means something quite different from past revolutionary clashes in Petrograd or rural China.

If we mean by revolution rapid and basic change, then the call of ethical theory and sociological reality is for total revolution. This is a cry for freedom and justice and peace. Not any one or two of them alone will do. This includes deliverance from economic deprivation and exploitation, but also from political tyranny and revolutionary violence. When Rap Brown suggested that violence is "as American as apple pie," he forgot that such justice, opportunity, and freedom as we have achieved is possible only because it is as American as hamburgers and milk shakes to reduce violence and to find better ways of dealing with our problems.

Whether violent or not, the "more militant than thou" posturing of politicians of polarization leads to an erosion of more moderate groups that are still the best hope of comprehensive, constructive change. It is particularly tragic when such moderate groups participate in their own demise. This they do by such an eagerness to maintain cordial relationships with extremists that they weaken their own independent programs, or by such a surrender to the pressures of extremists that they lapse into silence.

A polarization strategy is a major step on the road to totalitarianism. The theory behind it makes sense only if one is convinced that democratic change is impossible and that dictatorship is an acceptable outcome. On the twentieth anniversary of her "declaration of conscience" speech against Joseph McCarthy, Margaret Chase Smith said on the floor of the Senate: "Extremism bent upon polarization of our people is increasingly forcing upon the American people the narrow choice between anarchy and repression. And make no mistake about it. If that narrow choice has to be made, the American people, even if with reluctance and misgiving, will choose repression." [6]

When those toward the extreme left or right insist that dictatorship is a necessity for change, they are not revolutionary enough, at least within our society. They need to be reminded of how slowly regimes of the communist and fascist types have made any grants of liberty, and how thoroughly whatever economic improvements may have been made were poisoned by political tyranny and terror. Even fifty years of Soviet history produced almost no progress toward the extension of democratic liberties, as Alexander Dubcek and the Czechoslovakian people tragically discovered.

THE POLITICS OF UTOPIAN INTENTION

A second possible strategy expresses a type of perfectionism. It demands almost complete agreement with any person or movement before support is given. It withholds support from ambiguous persons or movements under circumstances where this makes it more likely that an even worse alternative will be successful. This action may be entirely innocent in intention, but it is a form of naïveté that is seriously destructive in its outcomes. This is illustrated in third-party movements that split the vote of the more desirable of two candidates, resulting in the election of the least desirable candidate. The same consequences follow from the refusal to vote at all in such an election. Refusal to vote for one side weakens that side and to that extent is effectively a vote for the opposing position. Because of their propensity for such utopian individualism, liberals have been accused of being the only known creature that eats members of its own species. This cannibalistic propensity is sometimes combined with the "single issue fallacy." Persons may be so impressed with the importance of one issue that they overlook a candidate's or party's position on others equally important. Some sincere persons in Germany were favorably disposed toward Hitler because he did not drink or smoke! This is much too simple a moralism to be considered ethical and much too innocent a political strategy to be considered realistic.

Sometimes there is a more sophisticated theory behind such actions than these comments have yet indicated. Under unusual circumstances a protest vote or withholding one's support may spur victory-hungry politicians to a more satisfactory position or strengthen the hand of more forward-looking factions within political movements. Such tactics become more constructive when there genuinely is no significant difference between the two candidates presented. Or, when there have been irresistible, undemocratic obstacles placed in the path of improving the position of a party, and the issues at stake in a particular election are not too serious, it may be necessary to ruin in order to rule—in the sense of gaining within the party the power to which one is democratically entitled. Or the results of this non-vote strategy are not so destructive when the most favorable candidate is sure to win big or to lose big anyway—although in this case protest also becomes more ineffectual.

The tendency of fanatics is to overestimate the frequency of such exceptional cases. Normally a utopian strategy is akin to Arnold Kaufman's "politics of self-indulgence." [7] This designation characterizes the action of those who avoid necessary compromise for the sake of their souls. They sacrifice the possibilities of political success to preserve their personal authenticity or integrity. Actually this becomes a way of losing one's soul. To protect one's "purity" at the expense of the poor is an immoral act. There is hypocrisy in this protest against hypocrisy. In a power struggle there are no sidelines. To withdraw or to be ineffectual is to strengthen the opposition. A mature ethics insists that we always note the plural consequences or unintended effects that flow from any act. The moral approach to decision-making requires that we do the best possible under ambiguous circumstances. In major controversies in a large society, choices are never unmixed. To refuse to do the best that is possible is to refuse to act ethically. As the economic buccaneer exploits by intense activity, so the dropout exploits by idleness or naïve perfectionism.

The good life includes calculation and essential compromise. These too are the calling of God to the creative man. It is not only true that by the best possible decisions the most rapid progress is made. It is also true that the finitude of the human situation makes it impossible to practice an unambiguous life-style. No one can completely dissociate himself from an imperfect world. If he thinks that he is doing so, it is only because he is closing his eyes to the ambiguities, which are nevertheless present in the actions he considers to be ideal. The moral response is to work creatively with ambiguity, keeping the tension with the ideal as tight as possible without overlooking the restraining realities within which we are compelled to make a choice.[8]

Utopian intention also often involves an unrecognized intolerance. On major social issues, society is composed of many small minorities, differing not only in position on a single issue but also in various combinations of positions on different issues. The only way that one minority can completely have its way is to coerce all others. Maximum freedom in this kind of society requires a measure of compromise. Those who refuse to compromise act as though others had no rights. Utopian fanaticism refuses representation to other groups in the complex consensus that emerges from free discussion. Insistence upon completely having one's own way assumes a degree of infallibility that no person has a right to claim. It is in a totalitarian society, as A. James Gregor puts it, that "the entire system is predicated upon the conviction that a minority of men possess a body of inviolable truth." Fundamental to such authoritarian ideologies is "an epistemology that precludes any substantial fallibility." [9]

THE POLITICS OF PARALLEL CULTURES

Those who despair of overcoming electoral opposition through usual procedures may also react by withdrawing and building alternate institutions within small groups. A dramatic shift in life-style is expected to provide a new society in microcosm. In a network of communes or in "free territories" in sections of the city or countryside, new patterns for handling economic and political functions are to be immediately practiced. These, then, will be available to commend themselves to the larger society as older institutions collapse.

There is something to be said for this approach, provided of course that the new patterns are actually superior. This method has been successfully used as a part of programs for social change. Gandhi, in his struggle for Indian independence, set up alternate structures for manufacturing cloth or making court decisions. The consumers' cooperative movement has built a distinctively different economic institution within a more traditional society. But neither of these withdrew from participation in other methods of change. Gandhi subordinated alternative structures in an aggressive total campaign. The cooperative movement maintains relationships with the total economic structure and is extremely active in education and in appropriate political matters. Better societies are not built in isolation from society or from the necessary processes of improvement.

Chief reliance on parallel cultures may be defensible where it is enough to introduce simple innovation or leisurely diffusion over a small area. More ambitious changes, however, cannot be made—or cannot be made fast enough—by this method. The attempt to do so leads to disillusionment. Where a shift of power and privilege is called for on a large scale or where vast, complex structures are involved, other strategies are essential. While parallel-civilization devotees are trying to grow enough vegetables, television broadcasting and "missile-rattling" continue in the rest of the world. A guru and his disciples ambling down a dusty roadway do not have a great deal of influence in a day of massive, immediate decisions. Continued life now depends on such things as a new foreign policy or alterations in the control of the structure of heavy industry. Alternate structures cannot provide parallels for all such points at issue. Withdrawal into building a more limited parallel civilization leaves worldwide life-and-death issues unaffected. Those who withdraw then become partly responsible for the continuation of present exploitation and for the breakdown to come. There is no way responsibly to avoid direct battle on all the complex major issues by withdrawing to a commune or a liberated neighborhood. No group can remain fully creative by detouring around the necessity of taking over effective power. Todd Gitlin criticized Reich's *Greening of America* for inventing "the myth of the painless revolution." [10] The gentle people cannot take over by simply living their own lives. We need to learn again from the Hebrew prophets, who saw it as natural and obvious to combine the witness of a personal life-style with political action. They made recommendations for domestic and foreign policy at the king's court, because they saw that God's battle for control of the world was being fought there. Absenteeism for them would have been a form of atheism.

The Politics of Complacent Gradualism

Another style of action is characteristic of those who are mildly concerned but also basically contented. They are so convinced that progress must come slowly that they move "with all the deliberate speed of a snail taking a nap." Complacent gradualism may be expressed as "benign neglect" of glaring problems. The moderate liberal is illustrating this by advocating limited changes that require comparatively little modification of the *status quo*. Those who practice this cautious gradualism have too little feeling of dissonance between accepted norm and actual practice. They have been too decisively affected by what Ellul calls "sociological propaganda." [11] With this term he describes the general climate of existing culture, which shapes man in its own image through customs and unconscious habits. The victim of such propaganda may make choices, but the choices are basically in conformity with his social environment. As Jack D. Douglas has put it, "Sociological propaganda is the real subliminal propaganda." [12]

In previous chapters I have presented evidence that we cannot deal adequately with contemporary problems without basic and rapid change. We shall have to make major choices in the next decade concerning the environment, international affairs, and the rebellion of the poor. Some basic problems are actually intensified by the extent to which we have begun partially to solve them. Arnold Kaufman calls our dilemma the "dialectic of disorder." [13] Our rhetoric of freedom and opportunity has kindled new hopes and aspirations, but our promises have not been matched by equally effective programs. Unfulfilled expectations consequently lead to frustration, anger, and a more militant revolutionary activity. To avoid still more violent and destructive action we must quickly close the gap between promise and fulfillment. There is no longer a halfway house. We become either activists against major evils or accomplices in them. Living a respectable suburban life, doing only a customary pittance for social improvement, and enjoying the fruits of exploitation without protest may be worse than shooting a man in cold blood, because it is helping to kill millions without any serious thought whatsoever.

In times of necessary change the conservative is the enemy. We recognize this in many a hard-fought election campaign. In times of rapid change the moderate liberal is also the enemy, because he is not willing to do all that must be done. One can miss a plane by driving away from the airport or with equal finality by driving toward the airport too slowly. From an ethical standpoint, omission is close to commission. Not to do good is to do evil. Not to do sufficient good fast enough is to do evil.

Inaction, or ineffective action, or delayed action are always deluding the supporters of change. Mild measures deceive us into thinking that we are doing something about the problem. Yet what we are doing is not enough to challenge the uncommitted or to inspire extraordinary support from those already committed. We ease our consciences but do not actually push on to what must be done. Foot-dragging is a long-standing device for defeating the cause one professes to serve. Particularly is this now the case when insufficient measures also contribute to the growth of extremist strategies of polarization. This becomes one of the consequences of weakening and immobilizing constructive groups nearer the center of the public-opinion spectrum.

It is characteristic of a time of rapid, progressive change that all the dividing lines in the spectrum of opinion ranging from radical to reactionary shift more quickly to the left. (During reactionary periods, the comparable movement is to the right.) In dynamic days, the radicalism of the past becomes the liberalism of the present. At the same time, many positions that were recently liberal quickly become conservative. The change formerly advocated has been adopted, and is now part of the status quo. Likewise, the conservatism of a few years ago becomes a reactionary stance today. For example, comprehensive national health insurance or world government were once radical positions. Now they are liberal. In a few years, at least health insurance may become conservative. Membership in the United Nations was once advocated by liberals. It is now the conservative position and the accepted policy of our nation, supported according to the public opinion polls by an overwhelming majority of the citizenry. Those who want to get the U.S. out of the U.N., and the U.N. out of the U.S., have become reactionary. Freedom of speech for dissenters, a social security system, or basic civil rights for racial minorities are all now conservative positions, guaranteed by constitution or law. The defense of thoroughgoing laissez-faire and opposition to all government economic planning was once conservative. It has now become reactionary.

If society is successfully to move through periods of rapid

change, those seeking improvement must go beyond custodial liberals, who are preoccupied with minor extensions of old-style liberal programs already partially adopted. More citizens will need to become radical liberals, pushing as hard as they can beyond the liberal programs of the past few decades in the conviction that conditions of "future shock" demand more rapid achievement of those goals as well as the adoption of new objectives with respect to the total quality of life.

A sufficiently sophisticated psychological or theological view of man should help us to understand our desire to pose as socially progressive, while at the same time we perpetuate private prerogatives. A favorite device of fortunate people is to pose as reformers in ways that involve no fundamental change. They put a liberal label on a conservative package, thereby perfuming existing immoralities. Or they pride themselves on being solid citizens providing a balanced conservatism, when they are actually reactionaries trying to turn history's clock backward. Those holding such positions may justify themselves as creative when in reality they are obstacles in the path of human development. The moving spectrum of public opinion leaves more Neanderthal men than we commonly recognize sitting in legislative halls, executive offices, or governing bodies of churches.

Even the best of yesterday's programs can delay the achievement of future goals. Right becomes wrong when it is not the best possible right, as the parable of the great feast should have taught us long ago (Luke 14:15–24). Mild activity inoculates us against adequate activity. All kinds of things can be used to reduce the intensity of one's insistence, including too much television, or alcohol, or sex, or spectator sports, or escapist religion. All these may become the opiate of the people. If one believes that the power of God is pulling us forward, he has a theological basis for holy impatience and wholehearted exertion. He gives up competing claims, including the convenience of verbalization as an escape. He knows that even right-sounding words may be a fraudulent form of cooperation with the highest he knows. He remembers the saying of Jesus, "Not everyone who says to me, 'Lord, Lord,' shall enter the kingdom of heaven, but he who does the will of my Father who is in heaven" (Matt. 7:21)—or the even more startling assertion, "The tax collectors and the harlots go into the kingdom of God before you" (Matt. 21:31). The latter statement was made to eminently respectable religious leaders. Scoundrels who repented were commended, while hypocritical pretensions of righteousness were condemned. In fast-moving times, the immorality of unimplemented intentions is matched by the futility of trifling gestures.

The Politics of Confrontational Coalition

The most effective strategy for basic change requires confrontation in a nonviolent sense.[14] Both the opposition and the issues must be confronted frankly, directly, and with specific proposals. To change entrenched attitudes of those standing between the innovator and his opponent, stronger inner dissonance must be created. This is "unfreezing," in the sense of loosening up the existing rigidity of fixed opinion. When persons no longer have the option of continuing to gloss over the issue, they more compellingly encounter the problem and the uncomfortable contradiction between their present position and their highest values.

This strategy calls for forthright statements, vigorous campaigning, and pressures toward decision. It is in this metaphorical sense that Jesus spoke of coming not to bring peace but a sword (Matt. 10:34). The kinds of changes that must now be made are disturbing to the biases of self-interest and the power of entrenched groups. Such groups will not accept with alacrity what seems to others so utterly reasonable. There are times when one cannot negotiate until he has compelled his opponent to come to the bargaining table. Situations must be created that impose deadlines for painful decisions that otherwise are too easily postponed. The problem of major change in a democracy is to persuade enough of a majority that by majority action they can compel dissidents to follow the social will.

Since, however, the whole point to the process is winning over instead of repelling those who lean toward supporting one's position, encounter must be restricted to such forms as are not self-defeating. The most effective confrontation takes place within a climate of understanding and acceptance of the opponent as a person. This is an essential part of the meaning of love. One had better make clear his points of agreement as well as of disagreement. At the same time that he insists upon eradicating poverty, a campaigner can make it clear that he also defends genuine values in present society and supports responsible maintenance of law and order. The opposition is not to be dismissed as blind or hopeless. It is important sympathetically to understand the complexities of their circumstances. This is being realistic instead of rhetorical. One can begin to communicate only within the range of experience and understanding of the audience. Any advocate of change must start where people are, knowing that there really is no other place to begin. People are bewildered, apprehensive, and frightened. Somehow we must bring hope and assurance as part of our challenge and confrontation.

In difficult situations we need to reemphasize Reinhold Niebuhr's statement that "the coercive factor in society is both necessary and dangerous." [15] A great deal of the danger can be avoided if necessary pressure does not threaten the essential being of the opponent as a person. Fortunately, there are such forms available. One of them is the kind of nonviolent resistance used by Mahatma Gandhi and Martin Luther King, Jr.[16] This asserts power in forms less likely to lead to backlash. It combines a maximum of persuasive power with a minimum of increasing hostility from the opposition. A more accepting attitude toward opponents as persons, along with vigorous opposition to unjust policies, adds up to a particularly potent presentation of a case, while at the same time keeping others comparatively more open to objective decision. It is also a method open to those who lack other forms of power. Through it, persons without status can vote with their feet and persuade through their pain. Demonstrations may become new forms of expression for those who do not own television stations.

Both Gandhi and King saw that such methods should be reserved for major issues where great resistances were faced. If used too often, they tend to have diminishing returns. There are other methods for continuous confrontation. These include community organization, political action, and energetic, persistent education. Both educational theory and creative imagination can fill these with drama and impact. They can become the means for escaping from complacent gradualism into accelerated confrontation.

The effectiveness of this strategy is supported by coalition-building, or uniting, through democratic process, large enough groups to gain social ends. Confrontational impact assumes alliances limited enough in size to share agreement on the major points at issue. At the same time, without sacrificing essentials, coalition requires programs sufficiently acceptable to a variety of points of view to win their support. The combination of confrontation with coalition provides an expression of participatory democracy that allows a large place for rational persuasion.

In supporting the necessity of coalition for democratic change, mathematics are conclusive. Neither the middle class nor the upper class, nor business associations nor the labor movement, are a majority in this country. Blacks constitute about 12 percent of the population. Those advocating any single specific program for national health insurance or a strengthened United Nations are in a minority. Unless we settle for a dictatorship, there is no alternative to forming coalitions, working out limited compromises, and moving together to win additional support. The components for a progressive confrontational coalition will include the poor and the racial minorities in the ghetto, but also large sections of the middle class in suburbia. Just as the race problem is primarily a white problem, so poverty will more largely have to be eliminated by the affluent than by the destitute. The war against want is more likely to be won in Washington than in Watts, in Massachusetts than in Mississippi. Among the more fortunate is found the chief concentration of resources and votes and power to change things. Economic insecurities and threats are becoming so obvious and so widespread in their effects that we can expect some support for modifications not from the young and from intellectuals alone, but from the entire spectrum of society.

Among the ruling elite and the chief beneficiaries of any *status quo* there have always been those so rigid and blind to reality that they have been unable to make the accommodations necessary to their own survival. But there have also been other aristocracies that have managed their affairs more adroitly. In recent years, some wider social goals have become more important to the realization of the economic ends of the new technostructure. In addition, broader education and wider ranges of interest have introduced a greater appreciation of the problems of others, as well as a more reliable realism about personal or class interests. Rich men and nations are coming to see both the immorality of vast inequalities and also the necessity for either sharing part of their wealth or losing all of it. This will not eliminate the sharpness of the confrontation to come, but it will increase the possibilities for the coalition approach, which is the only realistic democratic alternative that remains.

Those who have become disillusioned about democratic or nonviolent processes have often insisted that no major change in power distribution has ever occurred in this way. The historical question thus raised is a legitimate one. Those who are ignorant of history are condemned to repeat history. The past can teach us a great deal about basic economic and political changes. We do not need to start all over again. Before taking a great leap forward, it is well to take a long look backward. When we do this, we are compelled to say that almost all revolutionary social changes in Western history came through violent polarization. This is not surprising, since the resources of recent social invention and democratic process were, of course, not available during earlier centuries. We look at history, not with the expectation that we will be confined to all its antiquities, but for guidance in improving upon the immaturities of the past.

There is one major illustration that is particularly illuminating in this way. The decisive period in the shift of power from feudal agricultural interests to urban industrial interests came violently in all the major countries of Europe except for England. There the critical turning point was accomplished in an essentially nonviolent and democratic manner, most centrally in the passage of the Great Reform Bill of 1832. One of the more fascinating opportunities of my life has been a study of this transition, including perusal of the Francis Place manuscripts in the British Museum. There was a small amount of scattered violence, as in the burning of haystacks, or the smashing of agricultural machinery, or minor riots. There was a threat of revolution, which supported the statement that England was "on the eve of the barricades." Yet reform leadership was successful in restraining major outbreaks, and the final decision was made by parliamentary action. At one of the decisive votes, Macaulay described the scene in the packed House of Commons at three o'clock in the morning. "It was like seeing Caesar stabbed in the Senate House, or seeing Oliver taking the mace from the table; a sight to be seen only once, and never to be forgotten." When the victorious vote was announced, "the jaw of Peel fell; and the face of Twiss was as the face of a damned soul; and Herries looking like Judas taking his necktie off for the last operation." When the doors were opened, "all the passages, and the stairs into the waiting-rooms, were thronged by people who had waited until four in the morning to know the issue. We passed through a narrow lane between two thick masses of them; and all the way down they were shouting and waving their hats, till we got into the open air." [17]

Comparable to the storming of the Bastille or the capture of the Winter Palace of the Czars, nonviolent revolution also has its dramatic moments.

Several factors made possible this basic democratic change. For one thing, this had become an acute revolutionary situation, accompanied by economic distress and accumulated discontent. There was strong support for reform, and the threat of large-scale violence was evident. The reformers built an effective organization holding workers and the new middle class together against both conservative Tories and violent radicals. Leadership was energetic, effective, and imaginative as to methods. Numerous techniques were intensively used, including extensive agitation, demonstrations, and a variety of political pressures. Tactics included coercive elements, such as a limited amount of civil disobedience, strikes, withholding of taxes, or the run for gold on the Bank of England to prevent the appointment of the Duke of Wellington as prime minister. It is extremely significant that such a situation was created that the anti-reformers gave way before the forces of change, rather than resorting to violent repression. The king consented to create peers, and there was no later violent counterrevolution. It may well be that reports of guillotines elsewhere contributed to a willingness of the privileged to lose political power while saving their heads and some of their economic prerogatives. Undoubtedly there are other helpful factors in a transition of this sort, including the obvious necessity of change, the apparent futility of opposing the gathering tide of opinion and power, some overlapping of interests between contending parties, and the general ethos of a people supporting democratic and ethical values.

There have also been major crises in American history. During the presidencies of Jefferson and Jackson basic questions were raised about the nature and meaning of the new republic. Associated with Abraham Lincoln and his early successors were questions of national unity, the abolition of slavery, the impact of the industrial revolution, and of westward expansion.

Pressures for reform built up during the administrations of Theodore Roosevelt and Woodrow Wilson and reached their first climax in the presidency of Franklin D. Roosevelt. The issues involved acceptance of government responsibility for minimum individual welfare and opportunity, and for initiative in the development of the general economy. In the early stages of each of these periods there were sharp conflicts and divisions, so great that the country might have split apart. There was a violent rending of the nation in the Civil War. Apart from that, a new consensus was achieved on each of these matters, political parties did adapt or realign, and reasonably adequate programs were adopted. The third of these periods saw the rise of the labor movement, the passage of women's suffrage, the beginnings of the welfare state, and the civil rights revolution. All of these involved significant shifts in power alignment, and campaigns for them were all characterized by bitter conflict. Yet all were adopted essentially nonviolently, largely by processes of confrontational coalition.

The last of our important American revolutions is not yet completed. We have made basic shifts in direction, but poverty, waste, racism, concentration of control, and an outdated quality of life are still too much with us. No major American political group is yet giving bold leadership at all the fundamental points necessary for an unprecedentedly promising future. One might say that a new order in America has been born, with all its chief features present in infancy, but that it has not yet come into its adolescence in full voice and independent strength. Or to change the figure, we are still lumbering down the runway, not yet at the takeoff point. We would have to add that there is a barrier at the end of the runway, and that we had better pick up speed with the soundest flight plan we can devise.

This will require the best resources of all our major social institutions. In particular it is hard to see how we can make it without a vital church to provide a transcendent point of ethical reference and to reach a reasonable cross section of all ages, occupations, and regions in considerable numbers, with a message of impatience with avoidable evil and of complete commitment to greater good. In moving through their transition to industrialism and democracy, the British people had not only a Reformation heritage, but what has been called the second stage of the Reformation in the Quaker and Methodist movements. Apart from their specific teachings, both of these religious movements in their basic theological emphasis kept alive the doctrine of the calling. To this they added their comparable doctrines of the inner light and of perfection. At the same time that both movements were opposed to violence, they gave a religious impulse to the masses to win a new status. They provided a sense of dignity, latent strength, and dissatisfaction with an inferior position. In our day we are continuing to live through a major theological revolution that both preceded and accompanied our last social transition. Theologically this included the successive thrusts of the historical view of the Bible, the social gospel, the theological revival, church renewal, and current emphases on the secular and the future.

Insofar as these emphases are increasingly let loose in the general population, they would seem to be admirably suited to support the complex of basic social and economic changes now necessary. The pull of religion could also be intensified by the best aspects of our other social institutions. Added to this might be the increasing push of ever more obvious crisis. The combination may yet get us through this time of troubles and hope.

SYNTHESIS IN LIFE-STYLES

Strategies shaping the future involve changes in life-style, defined as the total complex of beliefs and actions that constitute our way of living. Changes in structures without changes in consciousness are largely futile. Likewise, changes in personal life-style without corresponding structural renovations and realistic uses of power produce no great social effect. In the early days of industrial society, the distinctive life pattern of the merchant and the manufacturer grew up within the milieu of feudal structures. With the development of capitalism the urban way of life superseded the rural. Now again distinctive new patterns are developing within the framework of the present order.

A useful way to think of the varieties now emerging is in terms of a dialectic movement from thesis to antithesis to synthesis. In other words, a first reaction to the outmoded is often an exaggerated pendulum swing to a drastic contradiction. The most dramatic of the latter antitheses is now practiced by a section of the "counterculture," which is not always confined to youth. The most promising foundation for the emerging future society is often found in a creative combination, or synthesis, of the best in both extreme positions. This can be illustrated in terms of four choices that have played a large part in our preceding politico-economic analysis.

One contest to be resolved concerns our basic method of production. At one extreme stand those who staunchly defend traditional technology. Enthusiasm about the exploits of industrialism blinds them to its person-destroying features. They hide the extent to which production of goods has been associated with dehumanization of man. They have built into their own life-style a full measure of the materialistic preoccupation that leaves us drowned in gadgets and suffocating in environmental pollution. They have not yet admitted to themselves that their unprecedented affluence brings too little happiness and too much air-conditioned misery.

The opposite reaction to this is a kind of romantic ruralism that largely rejects technology in favor of meditation and organic gardening. This idyllic ideology overlooks the fact that we could not fully develop other values in an economically undeveloped society. It is industry that has made possible our leisure and our longevity. So long as they want gasoline for their motorcycles, the anti-industrialists must accept intricate technological installations, distribution systems, and venture capital. The essential elements of a technical production process come trooping back in again. Either we become participants in the process or parasites on those who do. Complex technologies cannot be eliminated if we are to feed even a substantially lower population than we now have on earth. By using less efficient production processes, we participate in exploitation just as serious as that practiced by the imperialist who takes too much profit out of the colonies. Both are taking food from the hungry and homes from the homeless. It is shocking that some beautiful people are willing to exploit Madras for the sake of their own alternate society near Taos.

The critics of industrial technology are right in one respect. There is a promised land beyond the ranch houses. The defenders of an industrial society are right also. Any utopia, for the foreseeable future, will still include mass production of building materials. An appropriate synthesis would include a new spirit and revised structures in a person-centered technological society. This would retain the means for energetic and efficient use of human energy through machines. New elements in the synthesis would include a livelier attack on inhuman side effects of industrialism and altered goals for the economic process. Machines would become servants to a more modest standard of living. Planned technology would more consciously be used as a means toward higher values.

A second contest to be resolved between extreme positions involves the structure of social institutions, including the relationship of individual freedom to social control. On this issue the exaggerated rightist position is a form of institutionalism that, in practice, places the preservation of existing structures ahead of the function they were created to perform. We have already discussed at length the various ways that rightists dig in their heels against any important institutional change, even to the extent of autocratically stifling criticism. In many ways, ours is a sad scene. Conservatives underestimate the extent to which prevailing institutions feed on the persons they are meant to protect. They minimize the perils of bigness and bureaucracy and overlook ways in which full democratic participation is now denied to many citizens. In comparison with those more powerful, the weak have little to say about their own destiny. In both a nuclear and an ecological sense they may experience annihilation without representation.

Rightist extremism is often associated with an exaggerated laissez-faire individualism, in the belief that, by some kind of harmony of interest, selfishness also serves the best interests of the total group. They overlook the fact that such social anarchy, prematurely attempted, is transformed into autocracy. Maximum freedom requires enough social control to prevent individuals from imposing their will on majorities, with all citizens participating democratically in designing such controls.

The cultural extremists on the left would handle the problem of social structures by a kind of institutional bulldozing. Major existing organizations are regarded as hopelessly corrupting, meriting only demolition, in order that out of their ruins may grow unknown manifestations of the free spirit. A major ingredient of this position is the same kind of individualism and privatism that the counterculture has learned all too well from the capitalism it despises. Here is a similar strain of anarchism relying on voluntary cooperation and assuming a nonexistent harmony of interests among all individuals. This leads them, as it leads the rightists, into a strange and contradictory combination of theoretical individualism and actual centralization. While insisting upon doing one's own thing, they often conform to the styles and eccentricities of their own group as much as do junior executives at General Electric. This is often combined with a domineering intolerance toward those who disagree with their views. Nihilism always carries a touch of messianic pretentiousness, and it can also become moralistic, dogmatic, and dictatorial.

Extremists on the left do not sufficiently see the need for persisting social organization and control. Because there are serious conflicts of individual interests, freedom for majorities is often the fullest liberty possible in mass society. Because the streets belong to all the people and not just the street people, there must be police on the streets enforcing laws preferred by the total community. Because we want health care, we must have social structures such as intricately organized hospitals. Because we want freedom for a large population, we require democratic government. What would have happened to the Woodstock spirit if the festival had continued for a month, or without support systems? Even from the very first day, various incarnations of the "Woodstock Nation" are utterly dependent on those who ship and sell foodstuffs, or remove appendixes, or manufacture chemical toilets. It is sociological illiteracy to suggest that we can dispense with continuing institutions. Without such institutions we do not liberate full human potentialities. Unless there are some controls, we are not quite so free.

Instead of either structural ossification or annihilation, a more adequate social goal is more rapid and basic transformation of institutions in directions elaborated in previous chapters. Drastic problems now require major renovation, to be carried out while continuity of function is maintained. The planes have to keep running while we remodel the airport. Life-styles can include participation in more person-enhancing local units in big society and increased freedom in a wider pluralism. We can allow more anarchic liberties than custom or law have done, where these do not interfere with important social goals. There can be decisive improvements in the processes of democratic participation. Yet personal limitation by larger groups must be accepted wherever individual preferences seriously impede common purposes. In some areas even more such centralization is demanded than we have yet been willing to tolerate. This could even involve limited binding decisions on a world scale, if we want world peace.

As the first two aspects of life-styles involved social organization, the third and fourth relate to views of personal fulfillment. One issue here is the range of values to be actualized in the whole man. The diehard traditionalist accepts partial development, sharply limited by existing customs. His is a cheerless starvation of emotions, afraid to shout or dance or cry. He easily accepts the shallowness that may accompany specialization. His barren rationalism is pushed to the point of irrelevance. He neglects the world of nature for the concrete city. Acting as though pleasure was evil, he often postpones enjoyment so long as never fully to experience it. As a life-style, this becomes a chain postponing the liberation of a new humanity.

In opposing these anachronistic inhibitions, some ride the pendulum to the opposite extreme of hedonistic materialism. This emphasis is experienced as liberating, because it includes some values previously neglected. Yet it is still confining, because it also neglects the full range of potentialities of the whole man. In a sense there has been no fundamental revolt. The counterculture substitutes one form of materialism for another ("pot" for plastic) and one type of self-interest for another (private pleasure instead of private profit). The stress is still on lower values at the expense of higher, and on immediate rather than long-run consequences. The price for thin thrills and superficial sense-awareness is paid in the loss of more solid, durable satisfactions. Preoccupation with life as it might be lived on a Pacific island still leaves one something less than a human being. Nothing is gained in the move from giving sex too low a value to giving it too high a value. With sex or other physical values as the big thing in life, one gets to the point where all the encores are anticlimaxes. Boredom can then only be treated by distractions, since the medicine of more significant interests has been rejected.

A synthesis position intent on actualizing man's total potentialities would aim to remove inhibitions with respect to both the use of emotions and the use of the mind. While someone often needs to shout, "Stop intellectualizing," it is at least as important to suggest, "Stop emotionalizing." Carried to an extreme, physical spontaneity and intuition become a fascist-like thinking with one's blood. Reason without feeling may lead to useless and misleading outcomes, but unevaluated feeling easily produces treacherous conclusions, dogmatic intolerance, thoughtless cruelty, and misguided crusades. Man is more than cerebral, but the rational is one of his highest capacities.

Beyond that, life is not completely experienced without the ecstasy of spiritual awareness and insight into matters of ultimate concern. More important than improved products and intensified pleasures is the invitation to more significant perspectives. Beyond enhancing political power or groovy vibrations is meditation on the meaning of total life and the whole of reality.

The inclusive meaning of human actualization would include the extension of experience to the full dimensions just indicated. It would also learn much from the counterculture concerning the intensification of experience. Some things are not fully experienced until leisurely held and intensely seen. A glance out of a car window while passing a park is no substitute for lying half an hour contemplating the details of a tree. It takes concentration to find the meaning of the universe in the experiences of life.

Such extension and intensification of experience is impossible without examined priorities. Modern man is stifled by stimuli. To try to have everything is to end up having nothing. Some impulses must be denied to make other experiences possible. There is no more harmony among personal desires than there is compatibility of interests among social groups. The first notion is psychological naïveté, as the second is sociological obscurantism. Because extremisms have not said no to lower claims, they are not free to say yes to full human existence.

This has implications also for the continuation of fuller actualization through the longest possible ranges of time. Extremism among counterculturalists too often includes a prejudice against planning for the future, whether such planning takes the form of long-range programs for society or even the next two hours of a meeting agenda. Afraid in any way to predetermine the future, they overlook the fact that nonplanning also does just that. There is no way to avoid shaping the future by what we do or do not do now. By remaining uncommitted in order to be open to what the future may bring, we have already limited the possibilities in that future. The mistake is dogmatic rigidity, not dynamic foresight.

Also to be resolved is a second contradictory approach to the fulfillment of persons. For whom is the full range of values to be sought, primarily for others or for oneself? Is a life-style to be egoistic or altruistic? Even among extremists on the right, very few discard the rhetoric of altruism. Yet the prevailing practice is the direct pursuit of one's personal enhancement, and this is rationalized as the most effective method for aiding others. The self-made man not only controls an empire for himself, but, it is alleged, thereby he has greater influence for community improvement. This viewpoint insists that economists should assume that men will act in their own self-interest, and that foreign policy should never compromise the national interest. Though differently described for public-relations effect, the basic motivational drive remains acquisitive. Even such deodorized egoism quickly becomes exploitation. Its practitioners, for example, seem utterly insensitive to what the consequences for the poor will be if we simply continue our existing standard of living. Concentration on this kind of personal "fulfillment" has produced a very threatening society for racial minorities, the Third World, and all of us who live under the bomb and the smog.

Rebounding from a tense rush for private advancement, one reaction is a relaxed dropping out from social responsibility. Such counterculture extremists also have much to say about love and warn against selfish "ego trips," but their attempt to see a cop-out as a social contribution is as false a rationalization as the rightist extremist's justification of gross economic inequality. The defense attempted by dropouts is that theirs is a way of serving others by demonstrating an alternate society. But as was more fully discussed above, alternate social systems are not built in isolation from mass society or its change processes. Or, dropouts abstain from political participation, since no candidate perfectly expresses their full position. Thereby they comparatively strengthen the candidate they like least and would otherwise have voted against. This is politics played to lose, an effective support for the establishment.

Egoism can also be expressed as indolence. Counterculture extremists often "put down" the value of things that are difficult. Instead, they glorify easy mediocrity and make a virtue of inadequacy. This is an attempt to find personal identity without burdensome commitments and to express compassion without competence. Neither is possible. Both deprive society of the capabilities that some of its most promising members might have developed. At this point, self-styled loving people are incredibly insensitive to the cruel anguish that follows their neglect.

To avoid active aggrandizement on the one hand and passive inactivity on the other, a new human consciousness has yet to be built on the direct pursuit of the welfare of others. There really is no viable alternative left in international affairs except taking the interests of other nations as seriously as our own, and allowing the interests of humanity to take precedence over the interests of any single nation. In labor-management relations we have learned that optimum outcomes require that each group recognize the interests of the other. Corporations and labor unions can still learn more about subordinating their interests to the public welfare. Fortunately, many youth and some adults are becoming thoroughly impatient with our customary compromises in good will. We do not take love with radical seriousness until we give priority to others, with an even deeper personal happiness resulting as a by-product, rather than as a goal directly sought.

Now is the historical moment to develop a new consciousness moving beyond the wild swings of the oversimplifiers. A personal style appropriate to the next decades will integrate the elements spelled out above as the synthesis position on the basic issues discussed. Here is a life-style with emotional passion and intellectual clarity, reveling in sunsets and science and mystical experiences of God, expressing compassion that is historically and sociologically informed in effective institutional thrusts against war, poverty, and other major obstacles to a new humanity. Those living out of this consciousness refuse to drop out in despair or to destroy in desperation. They take radical love and total fulfillment much more seriously than does either extremism.

This kind of consciousness, which is in continuous revolt against existing cultural pressures, has always been the direction of thrust of man's highest moral and religious loyalties. The authentic Christian is a person who has adopted an alternate life-style. He follows a drastically different way. It is a caricature to picture the Christian as slightly more honest, gracious, and philanthropic than those who practice a respectable decency. Rather, religious faith pushes massively beyond anything like Charles Reich's Consciousness II and III [18]—or any corresponding representation in any other historical epoch. The seriously religious person accepts what might be called Consciousness n, using this symbol in its usual meaning of infinite extension. This is a moving goal that is constantly unrealized but always an actual potentiality.

REVOLUTION IN THE PURITAN ETHIC

In the minds of many persons, standing squarely in the path of a developing new consciousness is the traditional Puritan ethic. Consequently, the Puritan ethic is under such heavy fire today that it is hard to see how its flag can still be flying. In the attack on this formidable historical position, much has been said that is very wise and much that is very foolish. The difference, as in many other cases of confused identity, is often due to failure to make careful distinctions in definition. Is the Puritan ethic to be identified in terms of its original basic theological emphases or in terms of specific economic teachings that developed later?

In its basic theological insights the Puritan ethic is the Reformation or Protestant ethic. To be sure, even though the Reformers provided fresh emphasis and exposition, the doctrines involved go back much farther to a strong Biblical and Roman Catholic grounding. A central emphasis was on the transcendent sovereignty of God. This supported a continuously critical stance judging every human action and system. All idolatries were to be avoided and no relative value was to be made absolute. Therefore no economic system could be defended as the final expression of the Christian way. Any use of property was to be judged by the intentions of God for it. Associated with this was the emphasis on justification by faith. Salvation could never be earned. Man could never deserve what God gave him by his grace. This stood in opposition to all self-righteousness. Calvin reacted against the idea that a man prospered because of his own merit.

Related to God's call to salvation was his calling to secular activity. A man's religious vocation could be found in the layman's world of work as well as in the clergyman's field of service. This holy worldliness became particularly powerful since it was associated with intramundane, or worldly asceticism. Man was to work intensely, energetically, and prudently at his calling. He was to live simply and frugally in his consumption. It was this aspect of the teaching which made possible the accumulation of capital in response to the religious interests of man in the early days of capitalism, as communism has solved the problem of initial capital accumulation by compulsion, or as secular capitalists rely on self-interest or exploitation. This kind of specific application of a basic theological thrust made Protestantism a revolutionary impulse for its time, providing a necessary dynamic in the growth of capitalism and of the beginnings of political democracy. At that point in history this was a radically progressive step. As Michael Walzer has put it, the Calvinist saint was "the destroyer of an old order." Puritanism was "the earliest form of political radicalism." [19]

In some of the specific applications made of this basic theological position, particularly during later generations, the Protestant ethic became corrupted. Rasmussen calls this "the secularization of the Reformation." [20] This turned what had been a powerful revitalization of theological insight into a culture religion, sanctifying the practices of a particular way of life. God was no longer emphatically seen as constantly critical of all social life, but his judgments were largely confined to personal habits. Devotees of this business faith acted as though they earned salvation through hard work and business success. Their independent self-reliance became a form of self-righteousness. Adding dogmatism and rigidity to legalism made this a repressive system for many people. It tended to glorify acquisitiveness, or taking advantage of every opportunity for gain. Wealth came to be seen as a sign of the favor of God. The holy worldliness that had aimed to respond to God in secular activity became irresponsibly this-worldly. In all these respects the original thrust of the Protestant ethic was effectively contradicted. If this is what is meant by the Puritan ethic, then it needs to be rejected.

The perversions of the Puritan ethic, along with some of its more fundamental characteristics, have been severely criticized as inappropriate or even dangerous in modern times. Originated in an age of scarcity, it would no longer seem at home in an age of abundance. One line of attack on the Puritan ethic fastens on frugality, postponement of gratification, and thrift. Once men postponed gratification to accumulate capital. Now in a credit card civilization men postpone payment in order to gain immediate gratification. To do otherwise, it is argued, would lead to reduced production and system-wide depression.

A second form of attack on the Puritan ethic is made by those who object to its emphasis on work at a time when we can give heavier emphasis to play. This attacking party is partly composed of those who see progress as giving up work, or at least making recreational leisure the way of life, with work tolerated only insofar as it is necessary means. They would see the week as made for the weekend, rather than the weekend as a means toward better work during the week. The attack can also be made by those who still see a great need for creative work, but who are interested in a more playful spirit in one's creativity. They rebel against the somber, joyless approach that they associate with the term "Puritanism." They insist upon celebrating life, enjoying God's goodness, adding festivity and mirth to creativity and responsibility. In defining a man's productivity, they would add imagination to analysis, and spontaneity to routine. They are no longer willing dutifully to accept so many dismal conditions associated with toil, such as poor working conditions, subordination to autocratic supervision, or meaningless products. They are eager to enjoy the moment as well as to improve the future. They see no reason to postpone joy, since it can accompany work.[21]

Ethical conclusions about work and play depend on the definition of the two activities. If we refer to the kind of combination of celebration and creativity just described, then play is essential and is not contradictory to work. On the other hand, the playful life becomes personally and socially damaging if it becomes an all-absorbing, continuous search for shallow satisfactions in the easy and the trivial, or an escape from difficult and consistent commitment, or self-indulgence at the expense of productivity for human need. Every person has an obligation for social productivity. Persons with extended leisure, who spend all their time on the beach, soaking up sun and sex and food, are still drones and parasites. Under modern circumstances we need to be mightily achievement-oriented regarding human fulfillment for the dispossessed, or for world peace, or for economic justice. How can we consider that we are free to use self-indulgently the leisure that accompanies affluence, while most people in the world are dismally poor or grossly underdeveloped in social and spiritual quality? To say without qualification that we live in a society of abundance is nationalistic and materialistic. It disregards developing nations, as well as social and spiritual values which are very much in scarce supply here and abroad. To claim individualistic enjoyment of increased leisure too soon is to exhibit extraordinary insensitivity to the human anguish that results from our neglect. We cannot escape the message of the bumper sticker: "All the world is watching the United States, and all the United States is watching television." While we reject the compulsiveness associated with Puritanism, we need equally to avoid apathy.

Alert compassion would move us from a narrow concept of economic productivity to a broader view of socially productive activity. We might then pay salaries to students, mothers in the home, teachers' aides or social workers' aides, or friendly visitors to the neglected or the aged. When we see the full dimensions of social creativity, are men not working when they become music or art teachers for the indigent, social activists campaigning on major modern issues, drama directors in little theaters, ethical guidance counselors, religious researchers, or lay staff members of churches? It is still morally degenerate to do nothing for one's fellow man, but the list of what is something significant to do needs to be considerably lengthened. For those who genuinely love their fellow men, such kinds of creative work can be festival, as well as vocation.

An up-to-date list of characteristics of the vitally creative person contradicts the perversions that developed in the Puritan ethic, but it restates with novel emphases the essential features of the Reformation ethic of vocation. Social productivity still includes judging every system and our own lives by transcendent norms never completely realized. Life energies are to be vigorously and systematically directed toward human need in the secular world. This involves a kind of frugality in setting upper limits for our consumption. Limitation of gratification is necessary if we are not to plunder the earth in a form of piracy against future generations. Personal and family standards of living might reflect some form of functional simplicity, expending enough to carry on a creative life calling, but avoiding the luxury that robs the poor and the future while it expresses an outdated materialistic preoccupation. To change Veblen's classic phrase, the Christian should be characterized by conspicuous nonconsumption. J. Irwin Miller, board chairman of the Cummins Engine Company, recently told the General Board of the National Council of Churches that "the only way to raise the needed money to build systems needed to sustain civilized life in America is for citizens voluntarily to 'live cheaper,' and invest heavily in public expenditures." [22] This continues a form of Puritan frugality, but for different purposes. Private consumption is to be limited for the sake of massive public expenditures, to a great extent to sustain increased consumption by the poor.

The same transformation of purpose can be applied to the Reformation view of vocation. We are called to a rigorous, studious competence and to systematic, vigorous activity. But such personal energy at its best is to be directed toward a broader front of values and larger social purposes than previous generations considered important. Persons are to manage their occupational affairs in the public interest. The results will range from the fair employment practices and restricted income of the businessman to the sound craftsmanship and socially oriented labor unionism of the worker. Creative toil, whether for pay or during unpaid leisure, needs more often to include active campaigning for political solutions that by their responsible novelty match the tumultuousness of our problems. The new Puritan would avoid the full range of respectable cop-outs, from too much recreation to too little confrontation in personal witness.

The ascetic element in Reformation ethics is still appropriate in modern creativity, if it is interpreted to fit this historical epoch. Christian asceticism at its best was always positive rather than negative. It was fundamentally aimed at liberating the highest powers of personality from the blockage that would result from uncontrolled expression of lower drives. This asceticism of proportion emphasizes the need for personal priorities as well as national priorities. Some values must be given up for the sake of higher values. Personal comforts are seen as dispensable. One would be willing to face difficulty (e.g., social ostracism) or loss (e.g., lower salary) for the sake of a long-run social contribution.

The spirit of disciplined activity, if purged and modernized, is not then incompatible with the quality of a new humanity. Rather, it is indispensable to it. It does not leave dormant any important capacity, including the capacities for joy, aesthetic appreciation, human intimacy, and play. Rather, it awakens these and even infuses them into the experience of work. By relating economics and politics to ethics one makes his vocation an arena for creative growth as well as an expression of concern for human need, of hope for the future, and of devotion to the intentions of God.

Producing such a moral and spiritual transformation is the only way we are likely to pull through these critical times. As Michael Novak puts it, "The coming revolution will be moral or not at all." [23] We now need to complete one of the major changes of history to a more equalitarian society characterized by a new quality or style of life. Modern technology and interdependence make man's continuous propensity to evil even more ominous. Ours is a revolution against the combined threats of militarism, nationalism, materialism, egoism, and elitism. But we also have unprecedented resources in discoveries of the social sciences, and in the beginnings of the human potential movement. If we can now add to these the permeating penetration of love as reinforced by a modernized theology, we may provide a foundation for more thoroughgoing and rapid social change.

The words of Emerson are appropriate: "If there is any period one would desire to be born in—is it not the era of revolution when the old and the new stand side by side and admit of being compared; when all the energies of man are searched by fear and hope; when the historic glories of the old can be compensated by the rich possibilities of the new era? This time like all times is a very good one if one but knows what to do with it."

NOTES

CHAPTER 1. OPTIONS IN FUTURES:
I. A SUPER-INDUSTRIAL CIVILIZATION

1. Kenneth E. Boulding, *The Meaning of the Twentieth Century* (Harper & Row, Publishers, Inc., 1964), p. 7.

2. Quoted in Robert Theobald, *An Alternative Future for America II* (Swallow Press, Inc., 1968), p. 3.

3. Alvin Toffler, *Future Shock* (Random House, Inc., 1970). See also Herman Kahn and Anthony J. Wiener, *The Year 2000* (The Macmillan Company, 1967).

4. Arnold J. Toynbee, *A Study of History* (abridgment of Vols. I–VI by D. C. Somervell) (Oxford University Press, Inc., 1946), especially Pt. 2.

5. Toffler, *op. cit.*, p. 14.

6. Emil Brunner, *The Divine Imperative* (The Westminster Press, 1947), p. 247.

CHAPTER 2. OPTIONS IN FUTURES:
II. DISSONANCE AND DISASTER

1. Herman P. Miller, *Income Distribution in the United States* (U.S. Department of Commerce, Bureau of the Census, 1966), p. 21.

2. Herman P. Miller, *Rich Man, Poor Man* (Thomas Y. Crowell Company, 1971), p. 157. Compare Robert J. Lampman, *The Share of Top Wealth-Holders in National Wealth, 1922–1956* (Princeton University Press, 1962), noting his observation of

the statistical differences when calculations are based on families, which are the significant units for standards of living.

3. Henry Ehrlich, "Hugh Hefner's Jet Black Bunny in the Sky," *Look*, June 2, 1970.

4. Fred Sparks, *The $20,000,000 Honeymoon* (Dell Publishing Company, Inc., 1971), pp. 64–67.

5. Robert L. Heilbroner, *The Great Ascent* (Harper & Row, Publishers, Inc., 1963), pp. 23 ff.

6. For an economist's discussion of the perils of wealth, see Robert L. Heilbroner, *Between Capitalism and Socialism* (Random House, Inc., 1970), Ch. 2.

7. Gerhard N. Rostvold, *Financing California Government* (Dickenson Publishing Company, Inc., 1967), p. 82.

8. Joseph W. Barr, "Tax Reform: The Time Is Now," *Saturday Review*, March 22, 1969, pp. 22–23. Compare Robert L. Heilbroner, *The Limits of American Capitalism* (Harper & Row, Publishers, Inc., 1967), pp. 85–86.

9. Benjamin Ochner, "Middle Class Tax Reform?" *Trans-Action*, March–April, 1971, p. 60.

10. Joseph A. Pechman, "The Rich, the Poor, and the Taxes They Pay," *The Public Interest*, Fall, 1969, p. 33.

11. Pechman, *loc. cit.*, p. 43.

12. Frank H. Knight and Thornton W. Merrian, *The Economic Order and Religion* (Harper & Brothers, 1945), p. 114.

13. Karl Barth, *Community, State and Church* (Doubleday & Company, Inc., 1960), p. 173.

14. Reinhold Niebuhr, *The Nature and Destiny of Man* (Charles Scribner's Sons, 1941), Vol. I, p. 223.

15. Bruce Morgan, *Christians, the Church, and Property* (The Westminster Press, 1963), p. 76.

16. For a more detailed discussion of the relationship of Christian teachings to poverty, see Henry Clark, *The Christian Case Against Poverty* (Association Press, 1965), Chs. 1 and 2.

17. Irwin Ross, *Strategy for Liberals* (Harper & Brothers, 1949), p. 21.

18. *Time*, Feb. 2, 1970, p. 59.

19. See Paul R. Ehrlich, *Population Bomb* (Ballantine Books, Inc., 1968), pp. 149–151; Donella H. Meadows *et al.*, *The Limits to Growth: A Report of the Club of Rome Project on the Predicament of Mankind* (Universe Books, Inc., 1972).

20. J. W. Fulbright, *The Pentagon Propaganda Machine* (Liveright Publishing Corporation, 1970), p. 12.

21. Lester B. Pearson, "Trade, Aid, and Peace," *Saturday Review*, Feb. 22, 1969, p. 26.

22. Edmund A. Opitz, *Religion and Capitalism: Allies, Not Enemies* (Arlington House, Publishers, 1970), pp. 48–49.

23. Herbert Marcuse, *One-dimensional Man* (Beacon Press, Inc., 1964), p. 52.

24. Effective presentations of the two major points of view are Arnold M. Rose, *The Power Structure* (Oxford University Press, Inc., 1967), and G. William Domhoff, *Who Rules America?* (Prentice-Hall, Inc., 1967). For a specific joining of issues between these two positions, see G. William Domhoff, *The Higher Circles* (Random House, Inc., 1970), Ch. 9.

25. John Kenneth Galbraith, *The Affluent Society* (Houghton Mifflin Company, 1958), pp. 355–356.

CHAPTER 3. RESTRUCTURING THE FOUNDATIONS

1. Kenneth E. Boulding, *Beyond Economics* (The University of Michigan Press, 1968), p. 31.

2. Max Weber, *The Protestant Ethic and the Spirit of Capitalism* (Charles Scribner's Sons, 1930). Compare R. H. Tawney, *Religion and the Rise of Capitalism* (Harcourt Brace & Company, Inc., 1926) and Talcott Parsons, *The Structure of Social Action* (McGraw-Hill Book Company, Inc., 1937), Chs. 14 and 15. For different points of view, see H. M. Robertson, *Aspects of the Rise of Economic Individualism* (Cambridge University Press, 1933), and Kurt Samuelsson, *Religion and Economic Action* (Basic Books, Inc., Publishers, 1961).

3. Boulding, *Beyond Economics*, p. 198. For a similar theory from a modern sociologist, see Wilbert E. Moore, *Social Change* (Prentice-Hall, Inc., 1963), p. 75.

4. For favorable interpretations of this system, see Ludwig von Mises, *Human Action* (Yale University Press, 1949); Milton Friedman, *Capitalism and Freedom* (The University of Chicago Press, 1962); Edmund A. Opitz, *op. cit.*

5. Herman Finer, *Road to Reaction* (Little, Brown and Company, 1945), p. 173.

6. John Kenneth Galbraith, *The New Industrial State*, revised ed. (Houghton Mifflin Company, 1971), pp. 74–76.

7. Louis Turner, *Invisible Empires: Multinational Companies and the Modern World* (Harcourt, Brace Jovanovich, Inc., 1971), pp. 135–136.

8. Heilbroner, *The Limits of American Capitalism*, pp. 11–13.

9. *U. S. News & World Report*, July 19, 1971, p. 41.

10. John Kenneth Galbraith, *American Capitalism: The Concept of Countervailing Power*, 2d ed., rev. (Houghton Mifflin Company, 1956), p. 91.

11. Galbraith, *The New Industrial State*, p. 2.

12. Heilbroner, *The Limits of American Capitalism*, pp. 104–105.

13. Boulding, *Beyond Economics*, p. 47. On the military-industrial complex, see also Fred J. Cook, *The Warfare State* (The Macmillan Company, 1962); Fulbright, *op. cit.*; John Kenneth Galbraith, *How to Control the Military* (The New American Library of World Literature, Inc., 1969); Seymour Melman, *Pentagon Capitalism: The Political Economy of War* (McGraw-Hill Book Company, Inc., 1970).

14. William Blackstone, *Commentaries on the Laws of England* (Chicago: Callaghan and Co., 1899), p. 434.

15. R. H. Tawney, *The Acquisitive Society* (Harcourt, Brace and Howe, 1920). For a more detailed discussion of the concept of property in Christian tradition, see Charles Gore (ed.), *Property: Its Duties and Rights* (The Macmillan Company, 1922), and Joseph F. Fletcher (ed.), *Christianity and Property* (The Westminster Press, 1948), or the useful summary in Walter G. Muelder, *Religion and Economic Responsibility* (Charles Scribner's Sons, 1953), Ch. 5.

16. Thomas Aquinas, *Summa Theologica* (London: Burns, Oates & Washbourne, Ltd., 1929), Vol. X, pp. 232–233 (Part 2, 2d pt., question 66, art. 7).

17. Emil Brunner, *Justice and the Social Order* (Harper & Brothers, 1945), p. 59.

18. John Locke, *Two Treatises of Civil Government* (London: J. M. Dent and Sons, Ltd., 1924), pp. 130–131.

19. L. T. Hobhouse, *Morals in Evolution* (London: Chapman & Hall, Ltd., 1951), p. 608.

20. Morgan, *op. cit.*, p. 70.

21. Gore (ed.), *op. cit.*, p. xvii.

22. Pope John XXIII, *Mater et Magistra* (Paulist Press, 1962), pp. 39–40.

23. Fletcher (ed.), *op. cit.*, pp. 184–185.

24. Quoted in *ibid.*, p. 10.

25. Adam Smith, *The Wealth of Nations* (London: J. M. Dent and Sons, Ltd., 1910), Vol. I, pp. 13, 400.

26. Tawney, *The Acquisitive Society*, p. 27.

27. Boulding, *Beyond Economics*, p. 281.

28. See Douglas M. McGregor, in Warren G. Bennis *et al.*, *The Planning of Change* (Holt, Rinehart & Winston, Inc., 1961), pp. 425–426.

29. Friedrich Hayek, *The Road to Serfdom* (The University of Chicago Press, 1944), p. 36.

30. Raymond Baumhart, *An Honest Profit* (Holt, Rinehart & Winston, Inc., 1968), p. 121.

31. Reinhold Niebuhr, *The Children of Light and the Children of Darkness* (Charles Scribner's Sons, 1960), p. xiii.

32. For a more favorable exposition, see Robert Paul Wolff, *In Defense of Anarchism* (Harper & Row, Publishers, Inc., 1970).

33. This method of control in sound practice applies to major policy decisions. Actually, in a complex structure for making varied types of decisions, ours is a mixed political system as well as a mixed economy. Administrative decisions are quite properly made autocratically, within a framework of democratically determined policy. Freedom of expression and other comparable civil liberties are in a real sense an expression of anarchy.

34. Eugen Weber, *Varieties of Fascism* (D. Van Nostrand Company, Inc., 1964), p. 139.

35. Angelo Del Boca and Mario Giovana, *Fascism Today* (Random House, Inc., 1969), p. 1.

36. See T. W. Adorno *et al.*, *The Authoritarian Personality* (Harper & Brothers, 1950).

37. For a more detailed discussion of extremism, see Seymour M. Lipset and Earl Raab, *The Politics of Unreason* (Harper & Row, Publishers, Inc., 1970); H. A. and Bonaro Overstreet, *The Strange Tactics of Extremism* (W. W. Norton & Company, Inc., 1964) and *What We Must Know About Communism* (W. W.

Norton & Company, Inc., 1958); Arnold Forster and Benjamin R. Epstein, *Danger on the Right* (Random House, Inc., 1964); Benjamin R. Epstein and Arnold Forster, *Report on the John Birch Society* (Vintage Books, Inc., 1966).

38. Jerry Rubin, *Do It!* (Simon and Schuster, Inc., 1970), pp. 145–146.

39. J. B. Matthews, "Reds and Our Churches," *American Mercury*, July, 1953, p. 3.

40. Clarence W. Hall, "Must Our Churches Finance Revolution?" *Reader's Digest*, Oct., 1971, p. 95.

41. Quoted in *Tempo Newsletter* of the National Council of Churches, Nov., 1971, p. 2.

42. Fred J. Cook, *The Nightmare Decade* (Random House, Inc., 1971), pp. 148–149.

43. Arthur R. Miller, *The Assault on Privacy: Computers, Data Banks, and Dossiers* (The University of Michigan Press, 1971), p. 3.

44. Rubin, *op. cit.*, pp. 127, 243, 213–214.

45. Franklin H. Littell, *Wild Tongues: A Handbook of Social Pathology* (The Macmillan Company, 1969), p. 65. For suggestions for dealing with extremist threats, consult Harvey Seifert and Howard J. Clinebell, Jr., *Personal Growth and Social Change* (The Westminster Press, 1969), Ch. 7, esp. pp. 186–190; Wayne E. Oates, *Pastoral Counseling in Social Problems* (The Westminster Press, 1966), Ch. 2; Overstreet, *The Strange Tactics of Extremism*, Conclusion.

Chapter 4. Directions for Decision

1. Galbraith, *The New Industrial State*, p. 32.

2. Hayek, *op. cit.*, pp. 56–79.

3. Eduard Heimann, *Freedom and Order* (Charles Scribner's Sons, 1947), p. 5.

4. Quoted in Robert V. Andelson, *Imputed Rights* (University of Georgia Press, 1971), p. 8.

5. Karl Mannheim, *Freedom, Power, and Democratic Planning* (Oxford University Press, Inc., 1950), p. 15.

6. Pope John XXIII, *op. cit.*, p. 25.

7. Victor Obenhaus, *Ethics for an Industrial Age* (Harper & Row, Publishers, Inc., 1965), p. 169.

8. Additional provisions might also be considered, such as guaranteeing freedom of scientific inquiry, of access to the means of mass communication, or of objecting minorities to work and to buy as well as to speak.

9. For a brief discussion of possibilities and problems in international planning, see J. Tinbergen in Denys Munby (ed.), *Economic Growth in World Perspective* (Association Press, 1966), Ch. 13.

10. Quoted in editorial in *The Christian Century*, Dec. 31, 1947, p. 1605.

11. For elaboration of a similar listing, see Robert S. Benson and Harold Wolman (eds.), *Counterbudget* (Frederick A. Praeger, Inc., Publisher, 1971), especially pp. xi–xxix—although this proposal gives only limited attention to greater equality, protection against concentrations of power, or a new quality of life. For a convenient summary of opposing arguments, see Friedman, *op. cit.*, especially Chs. 10–11. Friedman tends to take redistribution for greater equality of opportunity less seriously, to turn existing abuses into arguments against continuation of programs rather than for improving the programs, to be unwilling to solve weaknesses of isolated measures by more comprehensive though still limited government initiative, or to disregard the degree to which individualistic or anarchic forms become limits on the freedom of majorities. For a theoretical and theological background see A. Dudley Ward (ed.), *Goals of Economic Life* (Harper & Brothers, 1953).

12. Insofar as we adopt wage guidelines or controls, should these not modify the usual uniform percentage increase considered acceptable for all, in order to allow a larger percentage of increase for low wages than for high wages?

13. For a much more detailed consideration from an ethical standpoint, see Philip Wogaman, *Guaranteed Annual Income: The Moral Issues* (Abingdon Press, 1968).

14. Friedman, *op. cit.*, p. 192.

15. Kahn and Wiener, *op. cit.*, p. 61.

16. Michael Harrington, *Toward a Democratic Left* (The Macmillan Company, 1968), p. 135.

17. Charles Fager, "Experimenting with a Simpler Life-Style," *The Christian Century*, Jan. 6, 1971, p. 10.

18. Heilbroner, *The Limits of American Capitalism*, p. 53. Those economists who advocate a "no-growth" or "stationary-state" econ-

omy are stressing the need for restricting industrial production in order to reduce resources depletion and environmental pollution. A better term would be "selective-growth" economy, clearly indicating possibilities for growth in the service sector of the economy. This could continue to raise the standard of living in the sense of a new quality of life. For the stationary-state proposal, see Boulding, *Beyond Economics*, pp. 275–287, and Herman E. Daly, in John Harte and Robert H. Socolow (eds.), *Patient Earth* (Holt, Rinehart & Winston, Inc., 1971), pp. 226–244.

19. Edward H. Carr, *Conditions of Peace* (The Macmillan Company, 1942), p. 82.

20. There is no attempt here to deal with ethical dimensions of day-to-day decisions by individual businessmen or workers. Such problems are dealt with in my own *Power Where the Action Is* (The Westminster Press, 1968), and in Howard R. Bowen, *Social Responsibilities of the Businessman* (Harper & Brothers, 1953); John A. Fitch, *Social Responsibilities of Organized Labor* (Harper & Brothers, 1957); Thomas M. Garrett, *Ethics in Business* (Sheed & Ward, Inc., 1963); Harold L. Johnson, *The Christian as a Businessman* (Association Press, 1964).

21. Denys Munby, *God and the Rich Society* (London: Oxford University Press, 1961), pp. 122–123.

22. Friedman, *op. cit.*, p. 23.

23. For further information: Jerry Voorhis, *American Cooperatives* (Harper & Row, Publishers, Inc., 1961), or the Cooperative League of the U.S.A., 59 E. Van Buren Street, Chicago, Ill. 60605.

24. For the theory of countervailing power, see Galbraith, *American Capitalism*, especially Chs. 9 and 10. In relating this to my outline, keep in mind the question whether chain stores can consistently be expected to protect consumer interests as directly or completely as consumers' cooperatives could.

25. Harrington, *op. cit.*, p. 291.

CHAPTER 5. STRATEGIES AND LIFE-STYLES

1. Saul D. Alinsky, *Rules for Radicals* (Random House, Inc., 1971), p. 29.

2. Steven Kelman, *Push Comes to Shove: The Escalation of Student Protest* (Houghton Mifflin Company, 1970), p. 5.

3. Arthur R. Cohen, *Attitude Change and Social Influence*

(Basic Books, Inc., Publishers, 1964), pp. 16–22, 88–90; Ross Stagner in Elton B. McNeil (ed.), *The Nature of Human Conflict* (Prentice-Hall, Inc., 1965), pp. 56–57; Lewis Coser, "Some Social Functions of Violence," *The Annals*, March, 1966, p. 17. For a defense of militance in spite of backlash, see Herbert Marcuse, *An Essay on Liberation* (Beacon Press, Inc., 1969), pp. 68–78, but note the authoritarian position that *after* the new elite has replaced the old, the people may judge the new government.

4. Allen D. Grimshaw, "Three Views of Urban Violence," *American Behavioral Scientist*, March–April, 1968, p. 3.

5. For further defense of revolutionary violence on religious grounds, see IDO-C (ed.), *When All Else Fails* (The Pilgrim Press, 1970).

6. For the full text of Margaret Chase Smith's June 1, 1970, speech, see *U. S. News & World Report*, June 15, 1970, p. 46.

7. See Arnold Kaufman, *The Radical Liberal* (Atherton Press, 1968).

8. Bringing out the general political implications of this was a major contribution of Reinhold Niebuhr, as for example in Ch. 1 of his *The Children of Light and the Children of Darkness*.

9. A. James Gregor, *Contemporary Radical Ideologies: Totalitarian Thought in the Twentieth Century* (Random House, Inc., 1968), pp. 328–329.

10. Review in *Psychology Today*, Feb., 1971, p. 12.

11. Jacques Ellul, *Propaganda* (Alfred A. Knopf, Inc., 1965).

12. Jack D. Douglas, *Freedom and Tyranny: Social Problems in a Technological Society* (Alfred A. Knopf, Inc., 1970), p. 117.

13. Kaufman, *op. cit.*, pp. 13–15.

14. For a summary of a great deal of the supporting theory and for further implications for agents of change, see Seifert and Clinebell, *op. cit.*

15. Reinhold Niebuhr, *Moral Man and Immoral Society* (Charles Scribner's Sons, 1932), p. 20.

16. For further elaboration, see Harvey Seifert, *Conquest by Suffering* (The Westminster Press, 1965); Joan V. Bondurant, *Conquest of Violence* (Princeton University Press, 1958); H. J. N. Horsburgh, *Non-violence and Aggression* (Oxford University Press, Inc., 1968); Harvey A. Hornstein et al., *Social Intervention* (The Free Press, 1971), Pt. 6.

17. Quoted in J. R. M. Butler, *The Passing of the Great Re-*

form *Bill* (London: Longmans, Green & Co., Ltd., 1914; New York: Augustus A. Kelley, Publishers, 1963), p. 207.

18. Charles A. Reich, *The Greening of America* (Random House, Inc., 1970).

19. Michael Walzer, *The Revolution of the Saints* (Harvard University Press, 1965), p. vii.

20. Albert T. Rasmussen, *Christian Responsibility in Economic Life* (The Westminster Press, 1965), pp. 57–58. See Chs. 3–5 for a stimulating discussion of this entire issue.

21. See Harvey Cox, *The Feast of Fools* (Harvard University Press, 1969).

22. This summary is in the words of *Tempo Newsletter* of the National Council of Churches, July–Aug., 1971, p. 2.

23. Michael Novak, *A Theology for Radical Politics* (Herder & Herder, Inc., 1969), p. 15.

INDEX